ESPIONAGE BEHIND THE WIRE

ESPIONAGE
Behind the Wire

HOWARD GREVILLE

Woodfield

First edition, published in 2003 by

WOODFIELD PUBLISHING
Woodfield House, Babsham Lane, Bognor Regis
West Sussex PO21 5EL, England.

ISBN 1-903953-33-2

CONTENTS

DEDICATION

I would like this book to serve as a friendly tribute to those fellow prisoners who did so much to make our lives more endurable. In those days it was a very new experience for the German and Austrian Administration to be confronted with British and Anzac POWs. The tricks, frolics and surprises that we produced straight out of the hat puzzled our captors and as a result we were often one step ahead in thought and deed.

Such activities may not have done much for the Allied cause but they were a great boost for our morale and some events like the burning down of the barracks, designed to segregate the "bad boys", must have had a potent effect on other prisoners such as the French and the Russians. My memories are firmly anchored with a great variety of personalities ranging from John (the Burglar), the accomplished boxer and dancer who led the burglary of the German clothing store, Sergeant Hector Smith of 6th Australian Infantry Division who played a leading role in the first capture of Tobruk, who sustained me in my hour of need and of course with the gallant New Zealander Army Captain who buoyed everybody's spirits and in Intelligence matters was my control.

ACKNOWLEDGEMENTS

I would like to thank my friend Ian Berckelman in Australia, who's efforts to find a publisher resulted in my story finally being published. My daughter Monica Foxwell also assisted in the publishing process.

I also drew on the writings of the following Authors: Professor Alan Bullock (Hitler and Stalin – Parallel Lives), David Downing (The Devil's Virtuosos – German Generals at War 1940-45), J.C. Masterman (The Double Cross System 1939 *-1945)* and Field Marshal Erich von Manstein (Verlorene Siege – Lost Victories).

FOREWORD

Taken prisoner in Greece in 1941 and later installed in an Austrian POW camp, Howard Greville was nevertheless able to obtain valuable military information, but more importantly, to have it immediately transmitted to England.

Military information obtained included details of Messerschmitt aircraft production, the location of German Battle HQ in Italy and other items. The remote location of the German chemical warfare plant was obtained and this information taken by the author to his Control. This entailed a rail journey, travelling with falsified papers pertaining to a sick man and accompanied by an armed German guard.

MI 9 and MI 19 instigated this field of intelligence. MI 9 was Military Intelligence while MI 19 was Escape Lines, headed by Airey Neave after his escape from Colditz. Neave later became a minister in Margaret Thatcher's Government and was murdered by the IRA.

Howard Greville has the ability to effortlessly captivate people with his charm and ready sense of humour. A born raconteur, he discusses exciting events in such a low key way they seem ordinary and it is only some time later one realises the actual difficulties endured to succeed in obtaining the information he sought.

As an ex member of the Australian Intelligence Corps it has given me great pleasure to read his tale and how he outwitted the German Gestapo.

Ian H. Berckelman AM

INTRODUCTION

When it became clear in early 1939 that the British Commonwealth was heading for war, civilians in Britain began volunteering to join the armed forces in ever increasing numbers. Because I was committed to taking an exam in German I delayed my application until mid summer, with a strong preference for joining the RNVR (I had been absorbed by British Naval history for many years).The training ship, President, on the Thames could take no more, however, so I decided to apply directly to the Admiral Commanding Reserves. I received from the Royal Navy a form which invited me to apply for a commission as an Acting Probationary Paymaster Sub-Lieutenant. Perhaps they were influenced because I was working as a head ledger clerk employed by a subsidiary of Unilever and I was also translating German correspondence.

Thinking this might involve pushing a pen in Scapa Flow, the naval base in Scotland, I pursued this line no further and turned to volunteering to join any of the well-known regiments in the City of London or the Essex Regiment which had a training centre near my home. All to no avail. In December 1939 I was conscripted into the Royal Corps of Signals and sent to Yorkshire for training as a wireless operator. The long training alternated with defence of the Yorkshire coast armed with a First World War rifle, 5 rounds of ammunition and a Molotov Cocktail to throw at an invading German tank! In October 1940 our unit left for North Africa.

Our troopship, the shallow-draughted Canadian Pacific liner Duchess of York, sailed in convoy from Liverpool for the long voyage via South Africa with a joyful break in Cape Town. All the while we were escorted by the Royal Navy except during a quick zigzag dash up the Red Sea when we were protected by the cruiser HMAS *Sydney*. She would have given a lively response to the shore batteries in Italian Somaliland had they dared to open fire upon us.

The signals company of which I was a member came under the command of General Wavell GOC Middle East 1939-1941. The command consisted of the 6th Australian Infantry Division (sometimes referred to, not by the British, as "Blameys Bludgers") and the 7th British Armoured Division (Desert Rats) – largely consisting of regular army troops. The whole force was often known as Wavell's 30,000. Given this small force with which to take on nearly 250,000 Italians, Wavell and his staff felt obliged to make it look a lot more so they sent dummy tanks, guns and planes into the desert. Wavell has been regarded as one of the founding fathers of disinformation and this was perhaps seen again in Greece where I was sent in March 1941 as a member of the 62,000 troops consisting of British, Australian and New Zealand units. The address I had to give my parents for writing to me was 1st Australian Corps of Medium Artillery. As a signals unit we had to maintain communications between the forward observation post and the artillery dug in behind. This artillery consisted of the 6th Medium London Regiment and the 7th Welsh Regiment. I knew of course that Australian artillery was in Greece in strength too.

The departure from Tobruk for Alexandria was an unforgettable time. This was on the first leg of the journey to Greece; members of my unit could volunteer to make the passage by sea if they so wished and I jumped at the chance upon our arrival at Tobruk harbour. I was a little surprised to find that we were ordered to board a small Polish freighter the Warsaw. Hastening to find out a little about her history I discovered that she was a clapped out 35-year-old ex British freighter of about 3,000 tons built by John Brown of Glasgow.

Anchored near us was the destroyer HMS Dainty and it was no great surprise to anyone when at dusk, the German Air Force attacked the shipping in the harbour. This attack was carried out by a squadron of Stukas (abbreviation of *Sturzkampfflugzeug*), the dive-bomber which in attack went into a near vertical dive with a siren howling. The multiple pom-pom guns of the Dainty together with the "Bushwhackers Artillery" of all Tobruk opened fire at once. The Dainty took a direct hit by a bomb in her magazine and on fire, broke into two sections and we heard there were few survivors. The old Warsaw was not hit but shuddered and trembled under the impact of falling bombs.

Next morning we left for Alexandria, making less than 10 knots, escorted by a tug armed only with a Lewis gun. It was a sunny calm day but we arrived unharmed.

Special Note

Throughout the narrative the prisoners of war on centre stage are natives of Britain, Australia and New Zealand. We became, for the Germans, one single entity and our food parcels, cigarettes and clothing were supplied by the British Red Cross. To allow the script to flow, I have very often used the all encompassing terms "we", "us" and "our". Where characters play a lead role they are referred to by nationality.

Howard Greville, England 2003

Figure 1: The Author, 1940s

AUTHOR'S NOTE

I was born in 1917 in Clapham, a suburb of south west London but was only 5 years old when the family moved to Brentwood, Essex, 18 miles north east of London. My father was an accountant with values that belonged to the Victorian era and he did not marry until he was 44. In his earlier days, there being no radio, TV and few motorcars, he became engaged in many varied pursuits which included painting in oils, singing with a voice trained by the London Guildhall School of Music, breeding and exhibiting chow dogs, photography, including his own developing and printing, sailing, reading on a very wide scale and making four elaborate bookcases in oak and his own crystal set when wireless was introduced.

I was educated at a minor public school in Essex, attending as a day boy. In my final year I was Head Boy, top in school and Captain of the 1ˢᵗ Soccer Eleven. Even though I always finished top in French exams I soon became convinced that German was the language to pursue in depth and therefore attended night school. As a child I grew up on Grimm's fairy tales and later read the history of the Great War of 1914-18 which included pictures of German officers in gleaming jackboots, cloaks and adorned sometimes with monocles. I was fascinated too by the Rhineland castles. In 1937 I went on a cruise on a German liner from London to Hamburg, all the time mingling with Germans. The reward was an intermediate certificate for German from the Royal Society of Arts. My obsession with the language was to determine the course of my life as the following narrative shows.

Figure 2: The Balkan region.

I   *Greece*

On the morning of 9th March 1941 HMS *Gloucester* approached the harbour of Piraeus carrying another eight hundred or so troops from Egypt. The sun shone brilliantly on the spectacular scene, with the colourful Greek islands dotted around in a vividly blue sea. It had been a fast and uneventful trip for us, the British Expeditionary Force of which I was a small part.

As the harbour came in sight the Band of the Royal Marines on board began to play and the atmosphere became more like that of a pleasure trip than of a military operation. As we drew nearer the landing stage I could begin to distinguish individuals among the little, colourful motley crowd which seemed to have assembled to meet us.

It was a time of considerable political confusion in these parts. Greece was at war with Italy (but not with Germany) and Britain was rushing a small force to the aid of the Greek Army. However, since the Italians, in spite of their supremacy in arms and numbers, were making little impression upon the stout-hearted Greeks, a German invasion to support the Italians was expected at almost any moment. At that time, while Greece was fighting with Italy, Britain and the Commonwealth were fighting their separate war with the

Axis Powers and our expeditionary force, small and inexperienced as it was, could ill be spared from the defence of Egypt to bolster the Greek defence.

It was ironic, of course, that though everyone knew invasion to be imminent, Germany and Greece were still officially at peace. Not only were the German Embassy staff still around, but were free to monitor the arrival of British, Australian and New Zealand troops in Greece. No doubt many of the Greeks who greeted soldiers with the Arabic greeting "Sahida" and who received such ready replies were petty informants for the Germans, sent to establish that the troops were indeed drawn from the Middle East and not from elsewhere. In a somewhat pompous 'security' lecture, we had already been warned to expect this sort of interrogation when we got ashore.

As we passed down the gangway I experienced a feeling of excited anticipation at the thought of landing in Greece. Left behind were the empty arid spaces of the North African desert, the sandstorms, scorpions, giant centipedes and also the detached unfriendly Egyptians of the cities. Those cities we had briefly visited at the beginning and end of our four month stay in North Africa. Egypt was of course supposed to be neutral and certainly the citizens there had never shown any regard for the British, in spite of the fact that we were keeping the Fascists out of their territory. Those four months in North Africa represented the sum total of my experience as a soldier on active service, and the same went for nearly all the rest of the company.

But Greece was different, Greece was Europe, with a totally different scene and different people; a gallant little nation fighting against tremendous odds with obsolete weapons yet scoring notable victories against the Italians. One could feel nothing but pleasure at the thought of supporting such a splendid people, and also it must be admitted at the prospect of exploring the city of Athens, of visiting the vastly impressive Acropolis, of standing in the shadow of the Parthenon and contemplating the might and splendour of the ancient world.

We thought there might be a chance of some good food and wine too, which certainly would make a welcome change from the monotony of the bully beef and biscuits which had made up such a very large part of the diet in the desert, relieved only here and there by tinned herrings or tinned meat and vegetables.

But from a military aspect we realised that the landing in Greece was in fact an attempt to secure a precarious foothold in Europe. It amounted to challenging the Germans on what was virtually now all their home ground – the Continent. Everybody in our little expeditionary force realised that this would be very different from the encounter with half-hearted and ill-led Italians in Africa.

HMS *Gloucester* was tied up to the quay. She was later sunk off Crete and her two sister cruisers *York* and *Bonaventure* were also sunk in the Mediterranean. Once ashore, loaded as we were with every scrap of kit anybody ever thought of issuing to a soldier, plus a rifle to show our warlike intent, we could look around and take in the scene.

The quayside presented the usual grey stonework with cranes, cables and odd gear littered around, characteristics of every harbour in the world; but stretching away into the distance was the rugged rocky shore, with islets here and there, lapped by the blue Mediterranean. This was indeed Greece. The few Greeks who were about gave us friendly smiles, and those few who could speak English expressed their pleasure at seeing us.

This Commonwealth force of British, Australians and New Zealanders did not appear to be expected in official quarters and our reception was a little disorganised! It was not known for certain where we had come from, where we were to go to, or what arrangements, if any, had been made for us. The Navy, seeing soldiers walking around looking rather like lost sheep, solved at least one immediate problem by providing a hot meal for everybody. Very large containers of a good meaty stew and vegetables were lowered over the side of the ship. By the time all the empties had been returned some idea had been arrived at by officialdom as to where we were to go and how we were to get there.

The Royal Navy had organised the transport of troops with dash and precision and we said good-bye to the sailors at the quayside with more than a tinge of reluctance. They little thought, at the time, and nor did we, that a few of them would meet up with us again under disastrous circumstances.

At this stage of the war the British-led armies had suffered a series of campaign defeats and the Navy had done much heroic work in evacuating our troops from Norway, France and Somaliland. It was only natural that in moving to the Greek mainland, some of those who had been evacuated after other campaigns should look back over their shoulders nostalgically to the sea, which to a large extent, was still Britain's undisputed highway.

Figure 3: Newly-arrived Australians share a drink with Greek troops at an outdoor cafe. (courtesy AWM.)

Personally, I was short of military experience on which to base expectations. But whatever our thoughts were at that moment, years in POW camps were not among the probabilities considered. From my observations capture was a contingency which British and Anzac troops rarely envisaged.

5

Some of our Army units spent a few weeks at Volos, near Athens, during which time equipment for the European theatre of war was issued. This, allowed us time for numerous excursions to the capital, to enjoy the many splendid attractions it had to offer and to be accorded a hearty welcome by the Athenians. There was an almost childish simplicity about the spontaneous warmth of their greeting. Smiles and handshakes came from all sides and occasionally flowers were tossed in the path of our army vehicles. Salutes between our men and Greek military personnel abounded. Rightly proud of their military successes, the Greeks looked upon themselves as worthy comrades in arms and upon the Commonwealth troops as sturdy allies who had come to help them through their trials. Cinemas and cafes echoed with ripe and derisive songs about Mussolini.

Finally, when all was ready for the road convoys to move up to what was to become the front line, there were wistful waves of farewell from the Greek population, particularly the girls, and flowers and garlands were thrown at the lorries.

Eventually our slender force of under four divisions, made up of troops from the UK, Australia and New Zealand and equipped mainly with 1914-1918 weapons, moved up to the north of Greece, with a tiny contingent from the Royal Air Force in support. There we awaited the German onslaught. We did not have to wait long; it came before dawn on Sunday, 6 April 1941. The Germans under Field-Marshal List deployed twenty-nine divisions and a complete

Air Fleet of about eight hundred operational aircraft, against the eighty of the RAF.

The best that the British-led force could do was to take as heavy a toll as possible of the enemy in the mountain passes and because of the vastly superior German armour, to endeavour to avoid any major engagement. This was not a comfortable introduction to the fighting phase of our military careers, but it had its moments!

Figure 4: Trucks winding through steep mountains in Greece.

For instance, one mountain pass was stormed by a German motor-cycle combination unit, whose main armament was a machine-gun fitted to the sidecar. These units were known to the Germans as 'Paradise Commandos' because of their high casualty rate and this one lived up to its name when it was picked off by an Australian Bren gunner. That small victory resulted in the welcome recapture of some of our white bread and famous 'Golden Syrup' found in the side car – both received with acclamation!

Unluckily for us the military situation grew rapidly worse, as the Greek Army crumbled under the irresistible weight of the German attack and fell back through our lines. They were accompanied by the remnants of the Royal Yugoslav Army, which had already suffered a major defeat in the German twin thrust into the Balkans. To add to the difficulties of our situation, the Bulgarian Army had moved up to support the Germans and were now on our right flank. The aerial bombardment became intense.

There were facetious comments from our ranks, about some of the puerile British propaganda of the day which wanted everyone to believe that the German war effort was based on a very short supply of oil. We were told that their tanks were made of three-ply timber sheeting and other similar nonsense, but as usual the Germans were highly efficient and quite adequately supplied.

Still we did not take things too seriously. Many excused the retirement of the Greeks and Yugoslavs with the naive reasoning that they were "foreigners, anyway". We had our lesson yet to learn!

We were soon reminded that this was to be a war with a new pattern. Our arms were old but the Germans had modern weapons and their Air Force in particular, pounded our positions from sunrise to sunset each day. They used every type of aircraft, including of course, the dive bomber – with its singularly unpleasant piercing scream. We were very vulnerable to air attack and I remember only one Bofors anti-aircraft gun in the sector; giving only nuisance resistance to the attackers. It was sometimes incredible to find, however, despite the most intensive bombing and machine-gunning, how light or non-existent the casualties in some target areas were. But the pressure was inexorable, and gradually the British and Commonwealth troops fell back to the sea.

Although not qualified to do so, I drove a 3-ton Bedford lorry with shot-up radiator that needed frequent refills. Carrying troops in the back and travelling mainly at night with restricted side lights I drove a route along a precipitous mountain road. Prior to our arrival, a mule train had been shot up from the air and I still remember the greenish eyes of the dead animals reflected in the dim lights.

After falling back to the coast, our Army units began destroying lorries and such equipment as was not of immediate use, and preparing for yet another evacuation by the Navy. This, because of German air supremacy, could only be carried out after dark. Night after night troops were evacuated from the beaches and taken either to Crete or back to Egypt. Each unit waited its turn with whatever patience and ribaldry it could muster. On the whole I would say that while the patience of those around me was adequate – in the circumstances really admirable – some of the ribaldry was even better. I remember, late one evening, just after sunset, creeping up to a vantage point that overlooked the sea. I could see, lined up on the beach awaiting embarkation, the grey shadowy figures of several infantry companies. The precision of their formation would have warmed the cockles of any sergeant-major's heart. Rejoining my companions I told them what I had seen.

"Oh for a big fat harlot and a box of chocolates!" said Paddy O'Malley from Perth, one of a number of Australians who had landed up with us. He said it with an air of resignation as we settled down to another night of waiting. That saying had become almost an 'evening prayer' by the time I met Paddy again in an Austrian POW camp.

Our so patiently awaited turn never came. It became clear that the evacuation could not be complete. Some units would have to be left behind, and soon it was evident that we were likely to be among the unlucky ones. Presently hope faded for our few hundred mixed troops in the olive groves near the village of Tolos on the coast of the Peloponnesian peninsula. We finally realised that the Navy had done all that lay in its power – and we were stranded ashore.

For our own defence, we did what we could, but it was exceedingly hard to dig holes in an olive grove, because of the thick root structure of the trees. With German aircraft carrying out machine-gun attacks at a daringly low level we found ourselves dancing a kind of maypole

10

round the trunks of the olive trees, seeking what scant cover the trees afforded from the circling aircraft. Then air attacks ceased and the German paratroop infantry closed in on our tiny remnant with German snipers taking their toll. On our side, both ammunition and food were desperately short and it was clear that the end must be near, but even then few of us realised what the end must be.

Figure 5: The embarkation beaches for the retreating British force. (courtesy AWM.)

The Germans sent over an emissary carrying a white flag in a captured British armoured car. He stated that his Commanding Officer knew our plight regarding the shortage of ammunition, food and water. The senior British officer was given an ultimatum, stating

11

that the choice was either to surrender, or failing that, the Germans would wipe us out and as an extra, raze the nearby village to the ground by air attack. So surrender it was, with a desperate last minute effort on our part to destroy or hide our weapons to avoid their capture by the enemy.

Prisoners of war! The possibility of such a fate had scarcely crossed the minds of most of those captured on that day, 28 April, 1941. Those who had thought about it, probably based their ideas on cinema images of the First War where soldiers leapt into the trenches with fixed bayonets calling, "Hands up!" Our surrender, nothing like so dramatic, was nevertheless inevitable and the only sensible thing to do in a hopeless situation. Yet it was a stunning blow. Secretly, nearly everybody must have felt as I did, an inward feeling of relief at being still alive. But what lay ahead? With Britain and the Commonwealth now entirely alone in the war it would be a long, long time before it was all over.

"I bet the Brylcreem boys[1] are knocking back pints in Alex (Alexandria) and laughing at us now," said one man.

"Old Chamberlain said that Hitler had missed the bus. He went by tank instead, it's quicker," was the comment of an Australian.

Contrary to what might have been expected in the circumstances, the Australians were not resentful toward the British Government or the 'Poms' around them. They were angry at what had happened without

---

[1] Nickname for 'spivs' and those avoiding service with the Army.

knowing or perhaps even wondering who was to blame. Some of them even felt that the Germans could have been beaten in Greece, but they did not know, of course, how great the odds against them were. They did not fully realise that the German Army was many years ahead in equipment, training and the general art of warfare.

Many harsh and unjust words were bandied around by the UK troops against the British Government for landing us in the scrape, and of course the RAF was severely blamed for lack of support. The only British aircraft seen in the last days of the campaign was a flying boat which came in to take off the Brass Hats, as high ranking officers were known, and had done nothing to improve the temper of the stranded troops. Soldiers could not be expected to be calmly philosophical at such moments, believing that they were "expendable" and that the ill-fated venture had always been bound to fail.

It was nearly dusk when the surrender took place. The Germans mobilized all available torches to search for the dead and wounded before the captives were marched to the port of Navplion. There we spent our first night as captives, without blankets and on the very stony playground of an unoccupied school. The evening air was heavy with the sweet scents of Greece in springtime, but we were in no mood to appreciate them. The bullfrogs, which kept up their chorus from several sides, seemed a more appropriate background as each man was lost in his own thoughts before sleep came to him. The German Swastika barely fluttered from the school flagpole.

The following morning the real sense of hopelessness set in, especially when no food was offered until after mid-day and then it was no more than a fifth of a tin of corned beef and one dry biscuit for the day. To add to our irritation and despondency we discovered that some of the enemy paratroopers guarding the camp were former members of the Czech Army. When I asked them why they were fighting for Hitler the reply was that the British and French had let down the Czech nation, so they were now fighting for "a New Order in Europe". There were certainly moments during the war when it was difficult to think of the correct retort on the spur of the moment. Our next move was by train to a prisoner-of-war camp just outside Corinth.

This was in a former Greek Army barracks but there was not sufficient undercover accommodation for the many thousands of prisoners who were gathered from all parts of Greece after the defeat. The majority had to do the best they could for themselves in the grounds. There were also some remnants of the Royal Yugoslav Army in the camp, their NCOs and WOs resplendent in their pale grey uniforms, with gold and scarlet insignia. The Germans had found that their Italian allies, although having played no significant part in the conquest of Greece, had started looting. Many Italians were apparently kept under considerable restraint in the camp. To the individual German soldier looting was strictly forbidden and many notices in German were pasted up on walls reminding the German soldier that the crime would be punishable by death. The "looting" of German-occupied territory was not the work of undisciplined troops;

it was a systematic procedure usually planned and carried out by the administration. It was set up behind the lines, and depended on the help of the Army.

The Italians in the camp adopted a lofty, victor's attitude towards us though they were little more than prisoners themselves and occasionally Berglieri alpine troops in their rather fancy uniforms and plumed hats would swagger through our lines – until they were taken down a peg or two. While their strength lasted, a few of the more belligerent of us would raid the Italian quarters at night.

Although the main purpose of these raids was to take it out on the Italians, there was an important secondary motive – to capture any spoil that was going, especially food or cigarettes. Some of the raiders I knew; two were North Country lorry drivers and two more were Australians. One of the latter was Shorty Stafford, a giant of six foot seven inches who was in the improvised or "Bush Artillery" which had defended Tobruk. In some of the skirmishing there he was reported to have fixed a bayonet to an anti-tank rifle which he carried as his personal weapon. How he managed to fix the bayonet and for what purpose it was intended is a matter for conjecture.

To carry out the raids, Shorty and his merry men would move through the centre of the compound, where there were no German sentries, to the Italian occupied barracks on the far side. Their movements were practically indiscernible in the black-out. Once upon their target, they would suddenly burst in upon a room full of Italians, yelling and laying about them and then just as suddenly withdraw, leaving their victims in panic and confusion and without any means of retribution. Because we outnumbered them, a counter attack on the British and especially the Australian "barbarians", as the Italians in Libya had sometimes referred to them, was simply not on.

The diet on which we found ourselves made it very difficult to keep up one's strength. Rations consisted of one large brown loaf for eight or ten men, and water from two wells in the camp. With the serious overcrowding, even obtaining water meant queuing for hours in the hot sunshine. The bread ration was sometimes varied by a cupful of rice, or a small portion of dried salt fish, or occasionally a very watery soup made with lentils which had sprouted an inch or two in length. As the days and weeks went by our physical strength ebbed away and dysentery and severe gastric upsets aggravated the situation. Eventually, very few prisoners had the strength to walk around unless it was necessary and few would even stand if they could sit. Soon even the most rabid anti-Italians among us had to resort to just calling down all manner of highly fanciful curses on their heads.

Being tall and naturally lean, my loss of weight was more noticeable. One Australian friend said I looked like an "undernourished greyhound", while another persisted in calling me "Atlas". Any kind of humour was relished in our otherwise unhappy state.

To add to the general desolate feeling, we were at this time entirely cut off regarding news and had no inkling of what was going on in the outside world. There were not even any German news bulletins. I suppose it was natural enough that, having no news, we took our small disaster to be indicative of the general course of the War.

When the British soldier finds himself in unfamiliar circumstances he first learns what the new regulations are, and then how they may be circumvented. Presently, led generally by the Cockneys among us, we found it was occasionally possible, with the connivance of the patrolling German guards, to buy a little extra food from Greek traders. We used whatever money, usually Greek or Egyptian, that remained to us, or bartered valuables such as watches, rings, and then lesser items like fountain pens, wallets, cigarette cases or even sundry Army equipment.

One piece of equipment that was never disposed of was the steel helmet, the soldiers' best friend. The Tin Hat was far more than a head covering and with its lining removed it served as a cooking utensil. It was often used for frying the hard tack biscuits which were occasionally substituted for bread using small quantities of olive oil, sometimes acquired from the traders. In addition, the steel helmet had to serve as a daily wash-basin and an occasional bath-tub. As clothing could be traded for food, very few prisoners had more than what they were wearing, and with soap unobtainable, laundering was a great problem. Yet, in spite of their shocking plight, the POWs did manage somehow to maintain a remarkable standard of cleanliness.

It was now five or six weeks since any of us had had a square meal. The persistent hunger nagged and nagged. Every man of us became almost entirely obsessed by thoughts of the right food and plenty of it, and there was some competition as to who could compose the most exotic menu. I remember a discussion between a Lancastrian and a Yorkshireman on the relative values of the cooking on either side of the Pennines which still makes me hungry in retrospect! A significant change had also come about in topics of conversation. Women were hardly ever mentioned; which was quite a remarkable switch since they normally occupy a large place in barrack room badinage and conversation. Strict moralists could not, in fact, take any comfort from the change.

It is often said that the way to a man's heart is by way of his stomach and I do not doubt the truth of this in peace time conditions. However, if the stomach is empty, the heart has a very poor chance. It may not be generally realised, but the starving male animal, no longer virile, scarcely becomes aware of Women's existence. During those dejected days in Corinth prisoner-of-war camp, had the most attractive and scantily clad dancing girls been paraded before us they would have earned no more than a few glances. Our minds would quickly have reverted to thoughts of roast pork followed by treacle tart.

As one who had always been fortunate to take good food for granted I was astounded at my own obsession with thoughts of food. My own dream meal at the time was tomato soup followed by grilled Dover Sole, then roast duckling, peas and new potatoes, ending with half a dozen chocolate éclairs with cream.

With the overcrowding and general wretchedness of living conditions we prisoners quickly, and inevitably, became lousy. Apart from their capacity for carrying disease, lice are man's worst bedfellows. Our lice were the kind that live and hatch eggs in the clothing and come out at night to feed on the body and cause incredible discomfort and much loss of sleep. The most persistent hunting and the use of chemicals and curses on our part seemed all in vain. There were certainly those with middle class inhibitions who did not feel like admitting that they had lice upon them until they felt that the majority of people around them were in the same boat. There were also the competitive types oblivious to social stigma who boasted about the high figures of their "kill" amongst the folds and seams of their clothes in the first hunt of the early morning. Then there were the methodical ones who hoped as a result of their great perseverance and patience they would win their battle in the end but perhaps they did not know that the egg of the louse is almost indestructible.

The Germans, no doubt mindful of the fact that the louse is a carrier of serious diseases, decided on a vigorous course of action. Every single item of clothing was removed from each of us and given a prolonged baking. While this was going on we were disinfected on a nearby beach by a unit of the German Army Medical Corps. To clothe his nakedness on the march to the beach through the town of Corinth each man was issued with a piece of calico and a safety-pin. Many were able to employ the baby's nappy technique with good effect but those with larger hips, or perhaps a slightly shorter ration of cloth, were unable to do this and were compelled to wear a kind of very split skirt. On the march all modesty went to whichever of the four winds was prevailing. Spraying with some sort of disinfectant, followed by a very brief dip in the sea was general procedure before returning to camp and our disinfected clothing. But it was all in vain. The pests persisted, and it was indeed nearly a year before enough insecticide became available and our lice generally disappeared.

It is probably under conditions of privation and hardships that one learns really to appreciate some of the simple good things of life. It seemed to me at that time – and I hope I have kept it in mind since – that if one has a full stomach, a hot bath available and clean white sheets on a comfortable bed, one would be bestowed with more than half of the blessings that make for wellbeing and contentment. Gastronomic "castle building"!

Such was the mental activity of those early days, there was scarcely any other form of distraction. The only semblance of artistic activity of any kind amongst my immediate friends was to see who could whistle an aria from such and such an opera or a leitmotiv from a certain Beethoven sonata or symphony. One of the star performers in this "cultural" activity was Ted Harrison, a curly haired young man in the Royal Corps of Signals. He was a first class wireless operator, a skill often found amongst those with a good ear for music. Ted contrived in a variety of ways, by using his hands or by manipulations with a tin mug before his mouth to imitate a range of orchestral sounds. With his broad repertoire he was able to reproduce snatches from all kinds of music with extracts from Beethoven symphonies more in demand than anything else.

With morale at a low ebb and nerves jangling, all kinds of wild rumours went buzzing round the camp. None were too wild to be clutched at by those in despair; Churchill was going to send in the Royal Marines to release the prisoners before the end of May, or the Germans could not move the prisoners to Germany because the RAF had devastated their lines of communication. Another was that the British were invading Germany through the Baltic and the Germans would be compelled to abandon Greece for the defence of their Fatherland and to leave us all behind in doing so. Such were the stories that were told, and often believed, but those who could think seriously had a nasty feeling that this was going to be a long drawn out business.

Our chief purveyor and embroiderer of rumours was a slightly built, sharp featured, red-headed Northumbrian named Carter. He was of an excitable disposition and simply could not sit down and relax in the shade to conserve strength as most of us did. Instead he would be off into the hot Grecian sun to chat to someone about how long the war was likely to last. He would then come back to tell us an improbable story, half of which he probably invented on the way. It would have been unkind to have told him that he was relating a lot of nonsense and perhaps it was good for some of us to listen to some make-believe.

Ginger Carter had manfully struggled on the long trek in Greece with every scrap of military equipment that the Germans had permitted him to retain. Most of us had shed items, one by one, in order to lighten our burden but Ginger had other ideas. He believed that if the Germans ever succeeded in getting us to Germany, which in his mind was doubtful, we would find the country a raging battleground, invaded from all sides and subjected to a continuous hail of bombs from the air. Therefore he considered that only the best equipped man with groundsheet, blankets, water-bottle and so on would survive. But most of all he treasured his steel helmet which he felt might well save his life in the days ahead.

To make matters worse the Germans now began their invasion of Crete and a large proportion of their air armada passed over Corinth, a most depressing sight for us. After a bitter struggle in which the Germans suffered heavy losses, another British defeat was registered. Apart from the depression it caused, this campaign had another unfortunate and direct effect upon us. During the campaign some German prisoners were brutally treated by the Cretans, those misdeeds being mistakenly attributed to our troops. As a form of reprisal, the Germans ordered that our rations be cut. After a few days however, the ration of bread was restored to its former, still inadequate, level.

Towards the end of May the Germans organised rail transport to move prisoners taken in Greece to Austria, a journey which, in the prevailing conditions, took on average five days and nights. Progress was slow because of the single line and with many prolonged stops due to demolitions carried out during the previous British retreat. We were herded into cattle-trucks, usually fifty or sixty per truck, which did not permit anyone to lie down. With the hot sunshine, cramped space and prevalent illness, conditions were most distressing and more than one truck had to carry a corpse for a night or day. For those who were chronically ill, every effort was made by nearly all comrades to give them a little more space to stretch out. Items of clothing would be given up to provide the invalid's head with an improvised pillow.

It was on this journey that I first began, tentatively, to use the German which not long before I had learned at school. My knowledge at first was inevitably of a somewhat pedantic and literary nature, and I certainly was not equipped to cope with the dialects I discovered amongst the German troops. The Wehrmacht had made use of Alpine troops in Greece and many of these were of course Bavarians or Austrians with their own expressions and a broad accent. Hitherto I had exchanged only odd words with officers and guards as occasion demanded but in the present situation I was compelled to make every effort to draw their attention to special cases of illness and distress. The guards were unable or unwilling to respond to any such appeals. At the time my reaction was to wish my teacher was there to hear what spoken German really sounded like.

Although I did not realise the implications of this at the time, I had begun a career as an interpreter which was to strongly influence my life for the next few years. This start was to lead eventually to my association with anti-Nazi Austrians. Although my German was passable, it was of course quite inadequate for describing complex medical symptoms and in this matter I had much initial help, in the form of stage whispers, from my young friend Martin Goldmann. He was a young German Jew who had fled to England only a few years before the war and German was his mother tongue. I had previously advised him to drop the final N from his name to make it look less Jewish. He was small in stature and of slight build and had a generally un-athletic gait However, he had a happy disposition with an overriding desire for good living with wine, women and song very much in the foreground. Understandably apprehensive at being amongst the Germans again, especially in British Army uniform, he did not openly disclose his knowledge of the language, but he helped me a great deal.

The train would stop in the mornings and evenings and prisoners were allowed to climb out of their trucks on to the side of the railway line to stretch their legs. Guards with their firearms cocked kept a very close watch on every move. An extraordinary feature of these stops was that they were seemingly known in advance to the women of nearby Greek villages, who would approach the train from the opposite side to that on which the prisoners had disembarked and throw pieces of dry bread over the trucks for the starving prisoners to catch in mid-air if they could. The guards tried, with shouts and sometimes even shots in the air, to discourage this show of sympathy. Undaunted, the women always came with their bread, which the desperately hungry men devoured like wolves. No Greek men were seen, although it might be quite unfair to say they took no part in supplying the food. More likely the Germans would not fire on women, whereas they might have done so on any men involved.

Standing on the far side of the train, our eyes would be fixed on the roof of the truck waiting for the shower of bread to appear; then up would go a sea of clutching hands and then all down on the ground in a mad scramble to collect what had been dropped. Greece was a poor country at best, and suffered cruelly from hunger during the war. Only months after occupation, shortages were being felt. Even in normal times, Greek country folk existed to a large extent on a simple diet of bread, goats' milk, cheese, olives and eggs, so their sharing of food was doubly generous.

At one point in our journey the railway line was blocked, where the retreating British had blown away a slice of the mountain. As a result we all alighted and began a 30-mile march over the mountains and down to the town of Lamia, where we joined another train. In the hot June sunshine, carrying our few remaining possessions, we were in no condition to undertake such a trek. Drained of their last ounce of strength, a few collapsed and died from utter exhaustion.

Yet again, throughout that march, the women of Greece found something to spare for us on every possible occasion, appearing on the roads with scraps of dry bread, a few olives and even a cigarette or two, unwavering in the face of German opposition. It was a gesture that all those who remember it – and none who experienced it can ever have forgotten – must rank high in the records of human kindness.

Figure 6: Locations of prisoner of war camps in Central Europe during World War II.

26

II   *Somewhat Uncordial Entente*

At Lamia we were allowed a welcome washing of heads and burning feet under a pump tap. We had stopped in a small town near the shores of one of Greece's innumerable gulfs, but we now boarded the train again and the whole crowded, noisome, clattering rail jolting recommenced. The cattle trucks on this side of the mountains seemed even more cramped. Of course we were told nothing and our view of the countryside we passed through was restricted to an occasional glimpse from the 30 x 12 inch ventilation apertures at opposite corners of the truck. We knew we were moving up through the length of Greece, and we then turned westward, passing through Sarajevo – the place where the First World War was triggered. Next was Belgrade, where a brief stop was made at a rail siding.

Towards mid June 1941 we arrived at Wolfsberg, a small town set in the hilly country of the province of Carinthia in south eastern Austria. However, neither the town nor the countryside was for us. Our destination was Stalag XVIIIA, a prisoner-of-war camp for "other ranks" which had been converted from a former Austrian cavalry barracks.

The original Officers' quarters, which were not bad, were naturally occupied by the German and Austrian personnel, and the troopers' quarters were already filled by French and Belgian prisoners-of-war. So we new arrivals were dumped into the stables, which had been "prepared" for us by furnishing them with wooden three tier bunks, each with a straw mattress. Here I began to find myself very much in demand, translating German orders and putting to our captors prisoners' requests, particularly on behalf of the sick. The broad Austrian dialect spoken by many of the guards, was a considerable obstacle for some time, and the pronunciation of my schoolboy German required more than a little adjustment! Gradually other interpreters were discovered.

The French in Stalag XVIIIA had been there for many months and were reasonably well settled in, as far as prisoners can be. In one sense they were very fortunate, for to supplement the camp diet they were already in receipt of regular Red Cross food supplies and parcels from home, often including cigarettes.

In meeting them, most of us in our very low and entirely poverty-stricken state expected a sympathetic welcome and a helping hand. That is what we hoped. We did not get it!

It is true that the odd small act of generosity was occasionally seen, but from the first few hours it became clear that the French were predominantly interested in business. They sought to barter our last remaining valuables or useful articles for food. Watches, rings and fountain pens were the things they most coveted, though cap badges and webbing belts were also traded. As a typical example a good wrist-watch might eventually, after some haggling, go for a tin of meat, two loaves of bread, a couple of dozen dry biscuits and perhaps twenty cigarettes.

It is a very odd sidelight on national characteristics that many months later some of these valuable items were restored to us by the Germans who, we presumed, had made a swoop on the French quarters. The Germans circulated a list with descriptions of the recovered items, and invited anyone to put in a claim for a return of his former possessions. Where genuine, or even probable, claims were made, the ring or watch for example was returned to its former owner.

No one could truly describe the Germans as kindly captors, but in some respects they were curiously punctilious, even in the early days of capture back at Corinth. When we traded through the barbed wire with Greek hawkers the supervising German sentry would sometimes decide for himself what was just measure for the money offered by the prisoner. It usually meant that we received a little more than we would otherwise have been given. In another way, the German sense of fair play was to later manifest itself again.

There was a small but welcome improvement in our diet in the camp, as compared with that on which we had starved in Corinth. A small portion of brown bread, a teaspoonful of jam, or similar quantity of margarine, and ersatz coffee constituted breakfast and the other two "meals" of the day would be either cabbage or potatoes with perhaps a minute quantity of meat on Sundays.

Clothing had by now become a serious problem and the German solution was to issue us with clothing which they had captured in the various territories they had occupied in Europe. Sometimes the results were quite comic. An unusual outfit was provided by what was generally believed to be former Czech Army uniforms. These were dark green, close-fitting tunics, some of them with numerous small brass buttons which somehow made the wearers look like cinema attendants.

My own not-very-fetching dress was quite a League of Nations effort. Beginning with the feet, I wore Dutch wooden clogs; socks were out and the standard issue was squares of a soft material in which to wrap the feet. Then came Greek Army trousers and a pale blue single-breasted jacket fastened with large brass balls; this was generally supposed to have been a Belgian artilleryman's jacket from the First World War! Surmounting the whole was a rather high Greek Army forage cap. What was left of my British Army boots was repaired by camp workers, using wooden tessellated soles supplied by the Germans.

The German clothing store was a building situated towards the centre of the camp and was not normally overlooked by guards. One of my enterprising friends succeeded in forcing the lock and he and I then proceeded to "sell" clothing from the store for food. We had discovered that clothing was in rather short supply with the French and whether or not they knew how the clothing was obtained did not bother us. We were not concerned with the ethics of the matter, as we went about our profitable and health-giving business. Hungry men toss many scruples overboard.

My own circle of friends in these early days was drawn, naturally enough, from within my Company which had been almost entirely captured in Greece. A few had got away somehow and there were also some casualties. Several groups of friends naturally formed and although scruples scarcely existed in exploiting a source of food, it was rigidly accepted that any gains would be shared to some extent with one's friends.

A few days after arrival in Wolfsberg came the dramatic news that Germany was at war with Russia. After weeks of silence, except latterly for propaganda on the loud-speaker system plus announcements of German U-boat successes, here was something of immense importance. It started us thinking and talking – and revived our interest in the progress of the war – as nothing had done since our capture. Britain was no longer alone. That was good news, but many feared that Germany, having overwhelmed all opponents in Europe after a few weeks of battle, might succeed in knocking out Russia in a few months. Events were to prove that these fears were not unfounded. As we all know now it was, as the Duke of Wellington said about another of the great decisive battles of the world, "A damn close run thing."

It was surprising to see how many amateur strategists we had among us! Fellows like Australian sheep farmers and British factory workers, who one would not have suspected of having any knowledge of such matters, would argue volubly and with considerable sense for hours about likely developments on this new front. It was generally hoped, however, that the vast spaces of Russia would make even the mighty German army seem rather small.

About the same time, Martin Goldman and I, of the Royal Corps of Signals, and half a dozen others, mostly members of the Army Education Corps, were commandeered to help in carding the basic details of all the British and Anzac prisoners, for German and Red Cross administrative purposes. This took several weeks, since there were many trainloads of prisoners still arriving from Greece. This work was done at the Army Headquarters in the town and we joined a dozen or so French clerks who had already been engaged on it. Each morning and afternoon the mixed party would be marched down to the headquarters escorted by German guards. This event was not without an international incident. The French Army, in the van on these occasions takes a much shorter, quicker pace than the British forces. We found it difficult to keep in step, and, after initial attempts, gave up trying. It was Aldershot versus St. Cyr and although the guards protested and the French clearly thought that the British and Anzacs should keep in step with them, we were content to settle down to a ratio of approximately three paces to the Frenchmen's' four. To the well drilled German mind the parade must have looked a shocking shambles, which indeed was what we intended.

At the Headquarters the clerical work was done in a large office, with the British and Anzacs sitting at one end of a very long table and the French at the other. In charge of the party and working at a separate desk, from which he could keep an eye on all of us, was a warrant officer, an Austrian by birth. Every morning a senior German officer came round on a tour of inspection and as soon as he appeared the warrant officer would leap to his feet, give a cracking salute and then in a staccato voice make his report to the officer. In this he would give his name, the number of prisoners in his charge and what they were doing. As a preliminary to it all, he would call the prisoners to attention with a bellowed "Achtung!" It was obvious, as the days went by, that this military paraphernalia was becoming too much for the non French element in the room and ways and means were devised for robbing the occasion of some of its military dignity.

It was discovered for instance that there was a slight slope on the table and if pencils were left at a certain angle when the owners were called to attention they could be relied upon to roll along the table. The rolling produced an irritating background noise to the German voices, before finally dropping to the floor. For even better sound effects it was found that the forms could be knocked over with the back of the legs in jumping to attention. The German officer might at first have mistaken this for military punctiliousness on the part of prisoners. He probably revised this view in time but never said anything to us. The French found it all rather disturbing.

Another of our enterprises which caused some uneasiness among both guards and our allies was fruit gathering. The road leading from the camp to the headquarters was, like so many German and Austrian roads, lined with fruit trees. These belonged to the local council, as did the fruit which they produced. As the summer wore on and the fruit began to ripen we decided to help ourselves while on the march to work. The method devised was for each man to arm himself with stones before setting out and to hurl these into the trees ahead in the hope of knocking down some fruit, to be picked up as the column went along. This creeping barrage which preceded the Anglo-French column produced vociferous protests from the Austrian sentries. The French also were clearly most unhappy about it. But the odd apple or pear made it worth any disturbance which it might occasion to others. Our most effective marksman at this was a corporal of the Cheshire Yeomanry who could usually be depended upon to bring down several fruits. It transpired that he was in the top flight of local cricketers in his home town and had put in a lot of practice at throwing a cricket ball at one stump.

In spite of such differences in attitude towards the status quo many genuine friendships developed between us and individual Frenchmen in which discussions ranging far and wide took place. From these the general impression emerged that most Frenchmen did not rate Britain's chances of survival highly. For themselves they seemed resigned to some kind of new order in Europe, with the Germans playing the leading role. On reflection, one could not fairly criticise the French too harshly at that stage of the war. Apart from national temperament, a basic difference lay in the fact that France was beaten and occupied, while Britain was not.

As the months had passed the British and Anzacs sought every possible relief from the boredom and oppression of prison camp life, even if it meant arguing with our guards. By comparison the French showed a tendency to reconcile themselves to captivity and to endeavour to make the best of it, by making the least possible trouble for their captors.

As a result of our association with the French at work, Martin and I and about a dozen more Britons were invited to attend a concert given by the French in their camp theatre. This theatre was quite well set up, with stage, curtains, lighting arrangements and orchestra. This particular concert was to be a musical one for chorus and orchestra. With some astonishment, and apprehension, it was discovered that the programme was to be devoted mainly to excerpts from Lohengrin, and that senior members of the German staff had been invited to attend it. Wagner's more tremendous music of course demands the maximum from singers and orchestra and to attempt such a performance with very limited resources was a woeful mistake from every point of view, particularly as Wagner is by no means a musical Frenchman's cup of tea!

Furthermore, to add to the misery, the conductor of the orchestra, an original character from the French Military Academy of Music, gave a rendering of his own new composition, a march which he entitled the "Stalag March". By implication this was a composition dedicated in mind and spirit to the trudge of prisoners in German captivity. It was a nasty, nauseating noise. All in all, a Sunday afternoon better forgotten. As Martin commented at the time: "Fancy the Frogs serving up such Teutonic tripe. Something to remind us of the Moulin Rouge would be much more acceptable".

Towards the end of that summer of 1941 our life underwent a fundamental change. The first Red Cross food parcels arrived, causing wild excitement.

I suppose that the hundreds of thousands of Red Cross workers and supporters all over the world must often have lapsed into a feeling that their efforts were all rather remote and impersonal. I only wish I could convey to them what their work meant to us. The hardest and toughest of men sat around on the ground untying their parcels with the gleeful expression of little children examining presents from Santa Claus. Months on a basic diet of potatoes and cabbage in Austria, after the dry bread and biscuit in Greece, had caused a bad effect on health. A notable problem was a large excess of bodily water retention and even some cases of beriberi were reported. Now, with the good food in the weekly parcels, all prisoners felt a deep sense of gratitude to the Red Cross, and a return to better health and life within themselves.

Morale soared, physical strength came back at a very rapid rate and, as a sure sign of a return to near normality, minds became predominantly occupied by two thoughts – escape and women.

III   *The Russians Arrive*

In the early autumn of 1941 the first trainloads of Russian prisoners arrived in Stalag XVIIIA. They presented a shocking picture of the miseries of war. If we prisoners had experienced a hard time in the early months of captivity – and indeed we had – it was as nothing compared to what the Red Army prisoners endured. No sensible farmer would treat his cattle as the Germans treated their Russian captives. Many thousands, of course, had not been able to endure; they had died by the way. Forced to strip off in the open air for the inevitable delousing process, with the early autumn snowflakes often falling, they presented a spectacle of little more than walking skeletons.

In the Stalag the Germans at first relied to some extent on the seemingly better fed Red Army Political Commissars to maintain some measure of discipline. For the smallest offence the erring soldiers were struck in the face by the Commissars with a kind of short-handled whip with leather thongs and in similar fashion, some German and Austrian guards also weighed in. The death rate amongst the Russians mounted daily and the grim sight of cartloads of uncovered corpses being unceremoniously carried out of the camp

37

to mass graves, left one with a feeling of numbed sorrow and a firm belief that the Nazis would one day surely pay.

At meal times the Russians stood in huge, long queues for their meagre ration of cabbage soup. They could often be seen propping up their desperately weak comrades who were too ill to hold out their own mess tins. There were even occasions when the man so supported was already dead.

Figure 7: The village of Steindorf.

Naturally we British Commonwealth troops decided at once to do all we could to help the Russians in their plight, though what we could do was little. We drew up a plan. Rather than make individual donations, we agreed that as each man drew his weekly Red Cross parcel he should make a voluntary gift of clothing and one or two tins of food to a central pool, which was then given to the Russian camp leaders for distribution. Nobody declined to contribute, and

38

considering our very mixed origins and backgrounds that was rather remarkable – something some sociologist might get around to considering some time perhaps! We were able to do what we did because in addition to the Red Cross food many of us were now in receipt of clothing and cigarette parcels from home, and from our civilian employers. From these other sources various articles were also donated to the Russians.

Like ourselves the Russians were housed in the stables but they were wired off from us in a separate compound. This segregation was part of the German policy to prevent fraternisation between the Russians and us. The Political Commissars, their immediate usefulness to the Germans having apparently expired, faded quickly from the scene. The last thing that the Germans desired was to maintain permanently the communist doctrine amongst their prisonersof-war, so presumably the commissars were sent elsewhere, or otherwise disposed of. The new Russian camp leaders appeared to be ordinary soldiers of various ranks who had some knowledge of the German language and who acted as group spokesmen.

It was clear that the Germans desired to present the Russians, in their wretchedness and destitution, as an inferior race, almost as subhuman; and to isolate them even from other prisoners. Any show of Anglo-Russian solidarity, or even decent human friendliness, angered the Germans. Thus all contact with the Russian compound had to be carried out surreptitiously, but in spite of the difficulties there must have been few Russians who did not receive some token of kindness and fellow-feeling from our compound. Russian gratitude, invariably mirrored in their faces, also manifested itself in a practical way. They sent presents of pieces of craftsmanship such as small carvings, metal work or by doing odd practical jobs for their benefactors wherever possible. There was scarcely any opportunity for speeches of thanks since discovery of these exchanges by the Germans would have wrecked the whole thing. From our point of view, speeches were quite unnecessary.

Among the Russians there were all types: they had come from all over USSR, from Leningrad to the Crimea, from Mongolia to the Caucasus. Many from the western republics of the Soviet Union were tall and fair haired with strong features and a good bearing. By contrast the Georgians tended to be shorter, dark and rather swarthy with flashing dark eyes. Then again those from the far eastern reaches were the moon-faced Mongols who seemed to wear a perpetual expression of placid surprise, and perhaps were not really able to grasp all the aspects of their situation. Perhaps the manifestations of Western civilisation and culture – as displayed for them by Stalag XVIIIA – were a bit beyond their comprehension!

Probably two main reasons accounted for the swarms of prisoners taken in the early days of the campaign on the Eastern Front. Many Russians, and especially the Ukrainians, had suffered grievously under Stalin's rule and no doubt thousands of them looked upon the invading Germans as liberators, of a kind. Consequently they had not fought with any great resolution. Too late they found that in the

Nazis they had backed another very bad horse, although some of them did actually join the Germans in their fight against Stalin, notably under General Vlassov. The other reason which accounted for the very large numbers of prisoners was the fact that the first Russian armies were routed and many large units encircled, by the initial devastating onslaught of the highlyorganised and well-equipped armoured and mechanised German armies.

Conversation with the Russians was made doubly difficult, by the German measures against fraternisation, and by the language problem. Most Russians, however, seem quick to learn to speak a foreign language, if not to read or write it, and the German language was soon being used quite effectively in AngloRussian contacts.

Politics was a tricky subject and if we asked the Russians any pointed questions they usually ducked the issue. From what they had seen of the Germans as invaders the Russian prisoners were certainly convinced that there was another big devil in the world besides Stalin!

It could fairly be said that a firm Anglo-Russian anti-Hitler front was established in the camp. Persistently the Russians would ask questions of an economic nature about life in Britain. Invariably it would be framed by asking how long a British plumber or a builder or some other kind of workman would have to work in order to earn a suit, a pair of shoes or something else. When we gave an estimation, we could see that comparisons were being made mentally with the poorer conditions for workers in the Soviet Union. But, in my limited experience at least, they would not disclose their thoughts. Clearly the MarxistLeninist dogma, which had taught them that all capitalists, including us, were enemies was still stuck firmly in their minds. Some aired what was probably a general belief, fostered by the Kremlin's propaganda, that Britain would in time turn and fight against the Russians.

But to whatever extent his mind may be captured by political dragooning, the Russian character and personality is unquenchable. Whatever they thought of us on a political plane, they recognised our friendliness and generosity as something very human and they responded to it with generous Slav warmth.

For his part the average British or Anzac soldier did not ponder deeply – or indeed at all – on Anglo-Soviet relations on the world stage, but simply reacted to the chap he could see, who, generally speaking, was a tot worse off than himself.

Ben Ryan, a Left Wing Australian journalist, well read in European history, summed up his views by saying: "These Ruskies are doing more than anyone else in fighting these Hun bastards. They are on our side and we should always be grateful to them for bearing the brunt of the war. But I reckon we've got seven years to wait before we get out of this place." Ben was sure that it would be the Eastern Front where the final issue would be decided. He believed that it would take years to reverse the tide there completely with the Germans having their strength gradually sapped away in a war of attrition.

Stalag XVIIIA was a transit camp and as prisoners were "processed" i.e. all their details listed and card indexed, so they were shunted out to working camps all over Austria. There was always a large number of more or less permanent "residents", made up of camp staff of all kinds, the sick, and those dodging the work column. By this time Martin was no longer so apprehensive about his Jewish background and with his fluent German became a busy interpreter. He relied upon his British uniform and the Geneva Convention to save him from persecution and it is true to say that though the Germans must have known, or at least suspected, that he was a Jew he was treated like the rest of us. He enjoyed a large measure of support from a violently anti-Nazi Austrian camp official named Stoll.

This was not so for the unfortunate Jews from all over Europe in the Palestinian companies which were captured in Greece. They were segregated, rounded up, and sent elsewhere, to what fate nobody knows.

The year 1941 produced a further shock, a rather personal one for the many troops who, like myself, had been ferried across from Egypt in HMS *Gloucester* for the ill-fated campaign in Greece. The cruiser was sunk by dive-bombers off the coast of Crete and, mostly in rags and tatters, the eighty-three survivors of a complement of nearly eight hundred arrived in Stalag XVIIIA. Among them were one or two familiar, indeed unforgettable, bearded faces symbolic of the Royal Navy. In spite of their ordeals the sailors were very good value and made a breezy contribution to camp life and especially to the camp theatre which had by then been established. It was a great disappointment to us when, after a few months' stay, they were removed by the Germans to a special naval camp, but true to their type their departure at least provided an amusing spectacle.

The Germans were generally finding that trying to instil discipline into the British and their Commonwealth chums was a very difficult and uphill task, not to say impossible. Saluting was almost non-existent and attendance at daily parades and working parties was quite haphazard. At roll-calls, turns would be taken to answer for many friends still in bed, and counting was made as difficult as possible by various devices such as switching to the back row after being counted in the front one.

Against this disorderly background the sailors' farewell parade was a supreme piece of blarney. Every piece of their equipment was either coated with Blanco[2] or polished. Boots and badges gleamed. Ordered to report at the Commandant's office near the main gate for checking out and to receive instructions for their departure, the survivors of HMS *Gloucester* marched with tremendous smartness from their quarters, preceded by their makeshift band playing Colonel Bogey and with a performing drum-major out ahead.

The Commandant, formerly an officer in the old Imperial Austrian Army, eyed their approach critically. He must have suspected the

---

[2] Blanco was a powdered substance applied to belts etc to make them look clean.

44

genuineness of this sudden punctiliousness – but when the company drew level with him and the Chief Petty Officer bellowed for an "Eyes Right", accompanied by his own super-smart salute, military courtesy left the Commandant no choice but to return it. Some of the Germans disliked the British servicemen while most tolerated us, but it is fair to say that of those we met not a single man ever completely fathomed our peculiar sense of humour. However, many Austrians could. The German mentality has a built-in resistance to ridicule, especially self-ridicule, and it was highly entertaining to watch their brushes with those of British background, who were always hell-bent on ridiculing their captors.

The clerical work concerning the registration of prisoners had now come to an end, so Martin and I and our fellow clerks found ourselves unemployed and with every intention of remaining so. For a while we achieved this by skipping the formality of attending any parades. Unfortunately I was caught in bed one morning by an Austrian sergeant-major, who did not let me out of his sight until I was dressed and had been marched down to the administration offices and assigned the job of interpreter at a working camp. This camp had already been established at Steindorf am Ossiachersee, a charming little village at the east end of the lake, from which the Dolomites could be seen on a fine day.

The fortunes of war were to separate me and Martin and other friends, but at least I was to be compensated by some very fine scenic effects!

IV *Labour Relations*

Figure 8: Some of the prisoners at Steindorf. Author 3rd from left back row, Dobbs 4th from lef,t middle row.

The prisoners at Steindorf working camp were much the usual mixture; being mainly from the United Kingdom, though with quite a few from Australia and New Zealand. We were supposed to be employed on renewing the railway track which led to Villach, near the Italian frontier. However, as might have been expected, the British and Anzac troops were neither model prisoners nor willing workers. We had no intention of doing more than we could possibly help, so friction and strife reigned on the site as it became a psychological battle-ground.

There was also a good deal of comedy, which helped the days pass for us. For instance, tools were often buried quietly and surreptitiously by the prisoners under sleepers, but nobody was ever caught doing this. Tools became scarce, though our supervisors never realised why! Indeed there came a time when crowbars were in such short supply that as a desperate measure the branches of trees were cut as substitutes, but of course these proved too pliable when used to heave the railway lines into position.

On arrival at the site in the early morning the Nazis amongst the civilian workers would meet their fellow Germans with the usual greeting "Heil Hitler!" – a substitute for genuine greetings at any time of day. To emulate this gesture and show it for the hollow thing it was, a few prisoners would hail one another quite solemnly with something similar, such as "Heil Churchill, George old boy!", or to be really provocative with the variation – "Heil Stalin"! The Germans eyed this performance with angry suspicion, but had no idea how to counter it.

With my arrival as an official interpreter, the camp saw the possibility of putting over all sorts of grievances to the Camp Commandant, regarding food and excessive work. The main protection for prisoners-of-war is the Geneva Convention; that is, of course, if the holding power is a signatory to it. Germany was a signatory, whereas some other powers, notably the Soviet Union and

Japan, were not. Unfortunately copies of the Convention could not be obtained for reference and most of us had merely been aware of its main provisions. These stipulated that prisoners-of-war were to be treated in a humane manner, given reasonable attention, fed to a standard equal to that of base troops of the holding power and that they must not be employed on "war work". What constituted "war work" and what did not, was a field upon which international lawyers had never reached firm conclusions. But of course some of our barrack-room lawyers knew all the answers.

One of the first things to be taken up with the camp officials was the matter of diet. The "heavy workers'" ration for prisoners – to which we were entitled on account of the heavy manual work we were supposed to be doing – contained some small variety in meat, vegetables and cheese, but potatoes made up a very large proportion of it. Without the Red Cross parcels it would have been totally inadequate for the work of plate laying. We took the reasonable view that it was not right that the Red Cross should supply the essential calories so that chaps could work for Hitler. Strikes and threats created a perpetual and terrific rumpus. The German reaction was either to try to drive us to the job at bayonet point, or to call in senior officers from the local headquarters to read the Riot Act, a procedure that was usually greeted with hearty abuse from our side, especially from the Australians.

There was an amusing sidelight upon this abuse, which was that the German or Austrian mind boggled completely at the amazing flexibility and all-purpose use of some of the more obscene and abusive words in the English language. They could not see how one word, fuck, could act, at different times, as a verb, adverb, adjective and noun. On being hard pressed for an explanation, I was both unable and unwilling to explain, but I did venture a vague theory that the English language had become enriched through its use in all parts of the world! And we let it go at that.

As the weeks went by it was decided to make a detailed list of the quantities of food given at each meal for each day. This we were able to do through the cooperation of the Austrian women in the cookhouse, who were very kindly disposed towards us British types and did their best for us with the rations issued to them. The plan was that after a certain time a demand should be made to see the local Military Commander, to lodge a formal complaint about the food and to show him the lists to back up the case. The main agitator for better food was the Camp Leader, Leslie King, an NCO of the Northamptonshire Regiment. He was not, in fact, a fellow with an enormous appetite and did not suffer particularly from our deprivations. However, he was representing the interests of his fellow prisoners and was determined to harry the Establishment on this score.

Technically we were the responsibility of the German Army, but we were on loan to, and employed by, the civilian contractors on the railway. In the struggle for better things it was necessary for us to drive a wedge between the civilians and the Army. The latter was considered likely to be more sympathetic towards our complaints. In dealing with German officers we found that we could occasionally benefit from that streak of Prussian chivalry which demanded honourable and fair treatment for the gallant, though vanquished, enemy.

As I began to feel my feet at Steindorf, and to take a closer look at my fellow-victims, I was interested to see how they differed from the general, unsorted, sample back at Stalag XVIIIA. There was the usual group of vociferous Australians and just a few of their milder cousins, the New Zealanders. Amongst those from the UK there were all sorts from regular soldiers to a solicitor's clerk who had just signed on for the duration. There were also two from Eire who considered that their privilege of being the enemy of the English had been usurped by the Germans and this had to be righted at all costs. And the way to do it was to fight the "divils".

When we had collected sufficient information about our diet we first approached the Camp Commandant who gave his support to the general proposal that it should be looked into. In his turn he requested that the local commander should visit the camp to hear our grievances. It was assumed that before getting down to business the commander would inspect the prisoners' quarters, and we well knew that nothing seems to please senior Army officers more than a smart turn-out. We decided that every effort should be made in this direction as part of a softening-up process, so cleaning and polishing and lining up of kit was carried out with diligence and all unsightly items concealed. For one brief day the spirit of Aldershot and Catterick hovered over Steindorf!

When the Commander arrived at the camp and walked round our living quarters escorted by the Camp Commandant, his face beamed with satisfaction, and he was generous with his compliments! He also took the unprecedented step of pointing out our smartness to the camp guards. They, being predominantly Austrian peasants, could somehow never contrive to look spick and span.

Then came the real business concerning rations, which was discussed in the Commandant's office. Our complaints were listened to patiently and the lists were carefully studied. Then the Camp Leader, Leslie King, and I were dismissed and the Camp Manager, or Lagerleiter, a badge-carrying Nazi civilian, was summoned. Being interested to hear the upshot of the matter we did not go far away. We went next door to our mess room, separated from the Commandant's office by just a single thickness of wooden wall. With an ear to the boards, I was able to hear a good deal – though once the Commander got going it was not necessary to strain my ears to hear. When he had worked up his anger with the civilian, he raised his voice to a terrific bellow! Loud and long he abused the wretched man for swindling the "English soldiers". Anyone who has ever heard a first class "bollicking" from a German officer will not readily forget it and for the hapless eavesdropper, as I was on this occasion, some of the outpouring was lost in the rising curve of the crescendos. Again and again he demanded account books from the civilian, to show what rations had been drawn and what had been issued. Hedging and stalling the Lagerleiter admitted that he had no books to show. Many of his remarks, however, were in a subdued and muffled tone so that we missed many of his replies.

Suddenly, however, we were treated to the astonishing and wholly delightful sight of the Lagerleiter being taken away from the camp by two policemen, who had apparently been summoned by telephone. Old Anni, the almost toothless Austrian cook, cackled triumphantly, and she was not the only one.

"What a beaut! Fancy, that Hun bastard's going to sit in the Boob for a spell. Wish I could send the rotten swine some rat poison!" This was the comment of Bob Carter, a hulking Australian and with an overpowering slap on my back that nearly gave me concussion, he added: "Good on you, Dolmetsch". This was the abbreviation for the German word Dolmetscher, or interpreter. I felt a little smug satisfaction at my enhanced standing, although it derived from a mere bureaucratic investigation but one which had ended with an unexpected dramatic scene.

It was subsequently learned that the Lagerleiter was convicted of misappropriating the rations, but, being a Nazi Party member, he was sentenced to only two or three weeks' imprisonment. After this very satisfying little incident the quantity of the rations improved but even then we did not consider them to be anything like satisfactory.

When working on the railway line the prisoners were split up into teams of three, each team having to remove a stated number of old sleepers and replace them with new ones. This was supposed to be done without interrupting the rail traffic, but of course we had other ideas, especially when the contractors incautiously demanded too much in the way of team output. The contractors, who were supervised by State Railway engineers, calculated that the number of sleepers renewed should be fixed at ten or eleven per day per team. One day they tried to force the issue, in spite of our heated protests, by stringing out the teams along the line at intervals of eleven sleepers. A go-slow was immediately decided upon as a countermove and I, having always flatly refused to do any other work than interpreting, took on the role of coordinator to ensure that roughly the same speed, or lack of it, was maintained by each team.

As often happened on such occasions a diversionary role was played by one of the great characters in our camp, Charlie Brown. Charlie was getting on for fifty and was one of "Blamey's Bludgers", the Australian Corps of older men set up by the Australian General Blamey to do Corps duties. Tall, erect, with a full light brown beard, he was the quietest and most placid of persons, never doing anything in a hurry and never speaking in anything but a slow, quiet manner. The German Commandant once said that he had a mental picture of Charlie back home in Queensland sitting under a shady tree, wearing a large sun hat, either dozing peacefully or puffing quietly at his pipe while he watched his plantation grow. When this was translated to Charlie he admitted that the Commandant's estimate was "about right". Never having exerted himself particularly on his own behalf, the very last thing Charlie intended to do was to do anything worthwhile for the Germans, though he was probably as fit and hardy as any man about the camp.

Because of his age he was given lighter odd jobs to do on the site, including the task of heating a cauldron of tar over a wood fire. The tar was used for coating the new sleeper bolts and, naturally enough, if the fire were too fierce the tar caught fire. The day of the go-slow provided Charlie with a situation which he had nicely "taped' and for which he was temperamentally perfectly equipped. He could usually be relied upon, quite unobtrusively of course, to let his tar pot catch fire at any really critical moment. The event was usually timed to fit in with some general moment of crisis or dispute or, alternatively, as a signal of welcome for the visit of some senior official of the State Railway.

As our slow motion day wore on it became more and more obvious that the allocated stint would not be fulfilled during normal working hours. The foremen and engineers became agitated and anxious, and not a little fractious, which delighted us! The track, where the old sleepers were still in place, was quite firm but intermittently where the new sleepers had been laid it was soft and spongy. A frightening spectacle was presented by the constant flow of huge locomotives which passed over these stretches, their enormous driving wheels rearing and plunging on the alternatively hard and soft patches. The sight was frightening to us laymen – but we also detected abject fear in the faces of the railway engineers, which was rather stimulating. To derail a train would have been a great prize for our go-slow campaign, but of course it might well have spelt demotion and imprisonment for the engineers in charge, so they were very unhappy indeed.

Figure 9: The town of Villach.

As evening approached, with the job not nearly finished, our trump card was played. We demanded our evening meal and quoted the Geneva Convention to substantiate our claim. Our demand was refused, uproar ensued, and Charlie's tar pot went up in flames in sympathy. One of the guards who were always on duty at the site was despatched to fetch the Camp Commandant to restore order and discipline. But unfortunately for the contractors after examining the situation the Commandant felt obliged to accede to our request for the evening meal. To the great dismay and indignation of the civilians he had us marched back to the camp. Furthermore he stated that he could not carry out his responsibility for our custody during darkness and so made it plain that we would not be returning to the site until next day.

As a result the engineers were forced to maintain an all-night vigil on the track, armed with lanterns to warn the night rail traffic of the dangerous state of the line. Thereafter the quantity of work allocated to us was greatly reduced and more or less, and somewhat precariously, more peaceful conditions reigned.

When the snows of winter fell, prisoners were all transferred to the dreadful, monotonous task of snow shovelling at Villach railway junction. It was one of Europe's coldest winters – quite the coldest for us – and temperatures sank so low that it became dangerous to touch anything metal with the bare hand for fear of it sticking. The hours dragged wearily by, the only relief being provided by lunch in one of the station waiting rooms which had been cleared of civilians and was reserved solely for the prisoners, railway foremen and the armed guards. The natural reaction after a stodgy lunch in a well-heated room was to fall into a sound sleep, and this we did to a man while the guards, of course, were obliged to keep awake and watch over us.

One day one of the prisoners, a small, quietly-spoken Yorkshireman by the name of Curwen, failed to rouse himself when the call came to return to work and one of the guards, a Sudetenlander, wakened him. This guard was a tall, knock-kneed man with a somewhat triangular, pasty face and deep sunk eyes and was generally known as "Death". He apparently gave Curwen a hearty shake which the latter, suddenly wakened, resented intensely. Leaping to his feet he drove a solid right-hander into the guard's face, knocking him flat on his back, his rifle clattering down with him. Then there was uproar.

Death, much to his credit, was on his feet in a flash and with two civilians leapt in my direction, and all three, sometimes alternately, sometimes together, shouted and raved at me, apparently as a means of retribution. I suppose they went for me because they knew Curwen would not understand them. My reaction on occasions such as this was to counter with some meaningless form of words, such as are used by Foreign Office spokesmen when confronted with really tricky questions. The reason I adopted this technique was not exactly lack of moral fibre, but in recognition of the desperate need to play for time while some of the steam went out of the situation and trigger fingers relaxed – they were armed and we were not!

Whilst all the bandying of words had been going on Curwen, the cause of it all, had calmly returned to his seat like a boxer returning to his corner after a knock-out in the first round. He ultimately collected no more than a severe reprimand for his part in the incident, which was an example of the tolerance sometimes exhibited by the German military mind.

Another occasion when our lack of inhibitions caused pandemonium was at the Christmas Camp concert, when the assembly began to sing that awful song "We're going to hang out our washing on the

Siegfried Line". The Commandant's reaction was to send in his guards with bayonets fixed to stop the song and to summon the poor old Interpreter for the inevitable lecture. While this was taking place the remainder of the company weighed in with "Land of Hope and Glory". This little episode was followed by lights-out at nine o'clock and an early parade in the snow on Boxing Day. All this may sound rather petty and trivial, but at the time it was not unsuccessful as a means of relieving the all-pervading monotony of prison camp existence. It was a curious life, but one which taught a high degree of self-reliance and made many recast their sense of values.

V   *A Bid for Freedom*

When the year 1942 got under way, escaping began to occupy the minds of a very large number of prisoners and when at last the warm weather came there was no shortage of entrants for what was known as the "Spring Handicap". Many and varied were the plans made and in all directions did escapers plan to go.

With so mixed a batch of humanity as we presented there was clearly no limit to what one or other of us might get into his head as a Plan. But within the realms of reasonable possibility our choice seemed to lie between Switzerland, whose border was over two hundred and fifty miles away, Hungary just over one hundred and fifty miles and Yugoslavia, the nearest point of which was under a hundred miles, but across hilly, wooded country. Although Yugoslavia was the nearest of our possible goals, we had no knowledge of what might be before us if we ever reached that country. We knew only that some tough fighting was going on there between the partisans and the Germans who had sent large numbers of troops. German security measures to repress news from that front were severe.

The feelings of the Yugoslavs were almost certainly friendly towards Britain, but they had more than enough to do to look after themselves, without helping us. Regarding Hungary, we had heard that a considerable portion of the population harboured pro-Allied feelings. This we felt was possibly true; whereas some unlikely stories suggested escaped English speaking prisoners-ofwar were being looked after by Hungarians and earning a living by such jobs as driving taxis in Budapest! The stories seemed highly unlikely, even though Hungary at that time certainly enjoyed a greater measure of independence than Yugoslavia. Technically, she was a German ally, not an occupied country.

However, to go East to Hungary seemed to be a step in the wrong direction, so Switzerland, in spite of the mountainous barriers, and the no doubt heavily guarded frontiers, seemed by comparison more promising. Our ultimate aim, ambitious though it may sound, was to land on the doormat of a British Embassy!

We were well aware that Switzerland, because of its neutrality, would demand our internment if we ever reached that country, but if one could escape from a German prisoner-of-war camp, surely one could escape from a Swiss internment camp? The distance and the terrain were, however, daunting. I had done a little pre-war hiking and was very conscious of the fact that one could cover only a limited mileage on a day's march and that only if well fed. On our anticipated ration for the attempted escape, we could not hope to walk all the way, so I came to the conclusion that we would have to do much of the journey by train – probably by coal train.

So our choice was never of an "easy" route; we well knew there was no such thing. Some of the less enlightened ventured eastwards towards the Soviet Union, with thoughts of "turning right" on the way, into Bulgaria and so into Turkey or better still Palestine, as it then was. So during this period of the war, at any time during the summer months, there were considerable numbers of exprisoners moving in all directions in German-occupied territory. Judging by their reactions the Germans became very concerned with this state of affairs. They really did try to put a stop to it.

As soon as a prisoner escaped from a camp, warnings were sent out to the ordinary police, railway police, field gendarmerie, frontier guards and the Gestapo. Dogs were often employed in the hunt too. Then to discourage us from even starting, placards were posted up in camps telling us that "Escaping is not a sport, IT WILL BE SHOT!" and warning that there were certain "death zones" where unauthorised people were liable to be shot on sight. Furthermore every camp received copies of a news-sheet listing those prisoners who had been recaptured and sentenced to the statutory punishment of three weeks in a prison cell on bread and water. But still they went, north, south, east and west, with perhaps distant Switzerland attracting the largest number. However, at this camp in Steindorf, no attempts so far had been made.

As might be expected, we had certain "Sporting Rules" to be observed in making an attempt to escape. No attempts were made when on any kind of privileged outing, such as a conducted walk, games outside the camp, or shopping expeditions. Nor on visits to local doctors or dentists. Had such occasions been used to stage escapes, there is no doubt that the privileges would have been at once withdrawn.

Consequently, any bid for freedom was most usually made from the camp itself, through the barbed wire, and at night, so as to gain the maximum start under cover of darkness. As a general rule such attempts were also made when the most unpopular or hated guards were on duty. This was because there was then a kind of bonus attached, as a guard on duty when a prisoner escaped was believed to receive a sentence of fourteen days arrest with loss of pay. There was however a certain amount of added risk attached to this practice since it was popularly understood that should a guard detect a prisoner in the act of escaping his instructions were first to call upon the prisoner to halt then, if this should fail, to fire a warning shot and then as a last resort to fire low to wound. It was reasonable to assume, therefore, that the most hostile and troublesome guards would skip or shorten the preliminary formalities and get on with the shooting.

It is amusing to remember a curious fact that throws an odd light on guardprisoner relationships. From time to time guards were posted from one camp to another camp, no doubt on the grounds that after a while they might become too familiar with prisoners; and probably for administrative reasons too. We, for the benefit of our fellow prisoners in other camps began a system of furnishing guards who were leaving with a written reference, which they would present to the Camp leader at their next posting. Indeed many guards were mindful of the fact that co-operation and peaceful co-existence with the prisoners was a guarantee of a reasonable life, whereas hostility or underhandedness could produce some nasty consequences.

As a result of this, a new guard on arrival might well seek out the Camp Leader at a suitable moment and present a reference which might have read as follows:

> *I am a completely reliable chap. You can trust me with your black market deals or to help in arranging meetings with girlfriends. Worth cultivating.*
>
> *(Signed .... Camp Leader).*

Once in a while however, other guards would pathetically present, with perfect confidence, something along the following lines:

> *I am a complete bastard. Underhanded, two-timing, do not trust me any further than you can kick me.*
>
> *(Signed .... etc.)*

In making an escape, there were a few basic essentials requiring special attention. Firstly, one needed a definite aim in mind and, as I have already suggested from Steindorf in Carinthia, Switzerland seemed to be the best bet, certainly so in 1942 when the situation in Yugoslavia was wildly uncertain.

Secondly, without personal knowledge of the whole countryside one needed a good map and some ideas on boardable transport, since trans-continental hiking for hundreds of miles through enemy territory was impractical. Also there was the need to take enough food to last at least a week or ten days and it was best for this to be of a light but highly nourishing nature.

The Germans were by now well aware of the fact that we were using the tinned food from Red Cross parcels to help in our escapes and accordingly they kept control of parcels and permitted the issue of only one or two opened tins per day. Often, however, it was possible to build up a hoard of unopened tins in the course of time, by the evasion of a few regulations. The issue of tins from the parcels took place in the evening and was generally an incursion on the guards' leisure time and they were therefore always in a hurry for the business to be over. Thus it was not difficult, with every man in the camp drawing something to eat, to use a little sleight of hand to obtain a few unopened tins.

During the summer I began to plan a break with two of my friends. One was Leslie King, the Camp Leader, who was a regular soldier and a corporal in an infantry regiment. To him, overcoming barbed wire was second nature.

Leslie, with his job as Camp Leader, like me as interpreter, was not forced to work on the railway and so, we were thrown together a good deal in carrying out general administrative duties in the camp. One of the things he had learnt in soldiering was how to cook a good meal and he prepared many tasty suppers in the evenings. In the hut he prepared meals from the combined resources of our two Red Cross parcels, the cooking being done when it was our turn on the stove. The contents of the parcels varied considerably so two people often combined in order to benefit from this variety. It was also economical to double-up since one tin was possibly too much for one man at a single sitting and left open its contents might deteriorate, whereas it would be eaten up in one meal by a twosome.

The other proposed escapee was Gordon Milroy, a New Zealand infantryman and a man of colossal physique. He was big, yet extraordinarily agile; probably both his balance and his power derived partly from his skill as a boxer. Gordon was a farmer in New Zealand and seemed to live only for outdoor pursuits. He had the vaguest notions about the geography of Europe, it was after all the other side of the world to him, and he badly needed a companion to map read for him in any escape plans. If, however, enthusiasm, determination and physical strength were the only attributes that were needed to effect an escape, Gordon had as good as gate-crashed on the Swiss already. I felt sure that only resolutely applied armed force would stop him once he was on the march. All three of us had toyed with plans for escaping and being a good trio we decided to throw in our lots together.

As always happened when a small group "paired up" for an attempted escape, our hut-mates were perfectly aware of what was going forward and did anything they could to help our preparations – while never asking questions or becoming involved in what we were up to.

There were no opportunities at that stage of obtaining civilian clothes from any friendly Austrians and for the general plan we were formulating our Army uniforms would have to suffice and indeed if we were recaptured, offer some protection under the Geneva Convention. Fortunately, new uniforms had been issued to us through the Red Cross, becoming available just after the first food parcels arrived.

We decided that one of the coal trains, which passed close by the camp and which frequently halted just up the line because of the single track rails, would provide the best form of a lift in the general direction westward. From regular observation and occasional glimpses of consignment notes it was ascertained that nearly all of these trains went down to Italy. That country, of course, had no coal and was therefore a burden on the German economy in that respect. Sometimes when the trains halted, some prisoners, if they were at work nearby, would clamber up the side of the trucks and grab the biggest piece of coal they could find for their camp stoves. If necessary, the coal would be shared with the guards for their stove and everybody would be happy, except perhaps Mussolini who got short weight.

A lift on a train to northern Italy would have meant useful progress, taking us beyond the borders of the Third Reich, to where there were not quite so many Germans. From northern Italy we felt we could plan again and perhaps even board another goods train in the direction of Switzerland. Crossing the frontier concealed on a goods train would have solved many problems. Alternative calculations were made for boarding a mixed goods train from Steindorf which might have travelled due west in Austria. We also realised that there were better possibilities of concealment under tarpaulins.

One of my tasks in the camp was to keep the wage accounts. Prisoners were paid in a scrip currency (the amounts varying between actual workers, and base camp staff who were paid less) and the money was used for gambling at cards or spent on shopping expeditions. This privilege was only allowed to be undertaken by me as Interpreter and one other prisoner, plus a guard. On Saturday afternoons we went to the village of Steindorf where we were held in reasonably high regard by most of the inhabitants. From some shopkeepers we often obtained useful items from under the counter – but food could never be purchased in this way.

At intervals the Camp accounts were checked by a German Army Paymaster who, I soon noticed, was incredibly short-sighted. With ordinary Germans only those who could not see properly were spared from the front line and this chap would indeed have been a menace with a gun. I also noticed that in his luggage he carried an excellent Wehrmacht map and as he was not able to see further than his nose it was no problem to remove it. On the pretext of going to the lavatory, I would pass the map to Leslie King who smartly got to work making a neat tracing of the main railways, roads, rivers and mountains of the relevant territory along the possible escape routes. The Paymaster's map was returned later in the day, its temporary absence having gone unnoticed.

During the first months of spring and summer our hoard of unopened tins of food was patiently built up and of course carefully concealed. The waiting period was not too trying, partly because the difficult Commandant who was in charge when I joined the camp had gone. He had proved to be a man of very uncertain temper, and was posted elsewhere – his replacement being a different character altogether.

Fritz Kachelmeier, the new one, was a short, plump, light-hearted Viennese and by no means an enthusiastic soldier. A peaceful time with a little fun and music thrown in were his fundamental requirements from life. He was, amongst other things, a very keen reader of George Bernard Shaw and liked to discuss his plays, but he could never understand why the British had not put Shaw in prison for the things he said about the English.

Often on the warm, still, summer evenings when the sun picked out the distant peaks of the Dolomites in a golden glow and long shadows stretched across the valley and glassy waters of the lake, the Commandant would play us his own music. Minus tunic, with army braces tensed, he would seat himself outside his office, surplus kilos drooping over the sides of the chair, at a spot which was very close to our compound and play his piano accordion. A gifted musician he played a wide variety of music with the lilt, zip and sense of rhythm which the Viennese have in such great measure. It was impossible, with the idyllic alpine scenery all round, not to sit and listen to the music whether one liked the instrument or not, without some fascination. The Commandant, between his various pieces, would gaze around at his audience and beam benevolently. From his general attitude he was called the Mother Hen, and was generally well regarded, even liked.

Another genial character worthy of mention at this stage was old Dr. Schwartz, physician and dentist, who lived in the neighbouring village of Feldkirchen. It was to this doctor that sick prisoners would report under escort and with myself always in attendance as interpreter. After giving his attention to the sick, and indeed he did give them his attention, he would dismiss everyone except myself from his surgery and then over a glass of brandy pass on the latest BBC version of the war news.

It was here that I again became clearly aware that many who had been incorporated into the Third (Thousand Year) Reich were strongly anti-Nazi at heart. The old doctor was indeed a splendid person. I vividly remember the night when a prisoner was suffering with suspected pneumonia, and Dr. Schwarz, after receiving a telephone call, was at the camp in a matter of minutes. He brought an ambulance to remove the patient to hospital and this was only one of the occasions when he proved himself to be a good friend and stout-hearted fellow.

However, these personalities are rather by the way. Leslie, Gordon and I had now decided that August would be the best month to make our attempt to escape. At that time, reasonably fine weather could be expected yet the nights would be a little longer than at midsummer. We did not intend to move during the hours of daylight, unless indeed we were well concealed on a goods train. One factor which helped us considerably was the strict German black-out regulations. Although not a single air raid alarm had yet been sounded in that part of Austria the faintest flicker of light after nightfall would cause a panic. In later years, when the bombing became intense, this black-out policy was reversed, many lights shone brightly until the imminent approach of the RAF whereupon master switches would plunge a wide area into darkness.

Our camp was surrounded by a double fence of barbed wire about ten feet high and this was patrolled at intervals by a guard. Although prisoners were locked indoors after dark, it did not worry us much, as we had no intention of walking out through the door anyway. The problem of cutting a hole through the barbed wire was not too difficult either, since Leslie King, also the camp cobbler, retained a pair of pliers which the guards were supposed to collect each night. There remained the problem of the noise of wire being cut and of avoiding the patrolling guard. We fixed the night of 12th August for the break out, in spite of its connection with the shooting season, partly because the weather was favourably cloudy and secondly because a much disliked guard was on duty. Being responsible for stopping us, he would collect a punishment if the escape was successful.

As a general rule whenever an attempted escape was made the individuals concerned could count on unstinting support from their fellow prisoners, and so it was with us. Ten o'clock at night was the time we elected to go, shortly after the final check-up on numbers by the duty guard. We would obtain the maximum start possible allowing us to exploit to the full the hours of darkness.

There are few things that we do consciously for the last time without some tinge of regret. I felt no reluctance at leaving the prison camp, but as I talked to some of my fellow prisoners before our departure, I was just a little sad to be leaving our small community once and for all. We knew that escaped prisoners, once recaptured were never returned to their work camps but sent back to Stalag XVIIIA, the distribution centre and then out to a different work camp. The life at Steindorf, restricted and irksome though it was, had never been without its lighter and brighter moments. Furthermore in this attractive corner of Austria the sun had shone often from a cloudless sky on the fine wooded mountains nearby. Captives and free men alike enjoyed the spring which had brought to the broad valley around us that wonderful haze of new green life and riot of colourful flowers. We all marvelled at the beauty and later autumn had brought the falling leaves and the whisper of approaching snow.

But to return to the immediate scene, the camp band undertook to keep up plenty of noise to drown any sounds that might alarm the guards. The three of us assembled in the washroom at the back of the camp. It was in this spacious room that prisoners washed themselves and their clothes – there being no baths of any kind. On odd occasions the Austrian kitchen maids had been known to pay a surprise visit and take a lively interest in what there was to see. To those of us with rather stodgy middle-class English backgrounds, this somewhat Continental approach was mildly surprising!

It was from this room that our initial exit from the quarters was to be forced. The windows were all fitted with steel bars, of course, but a screwdriver lifted from the railway tool shed was sufficient to free the extremities of some of the bars where they were fixed to the wall. Gordon Milroy then provided all the muscle power that was needed to bend the bars right back and so present an open window. Meanwhile a human chain of informers had been set up to report on the movement of the patrolling guard. The observer at the far end of the chain eventually reported that the guard was engrossed in conversation with someone at the opposite end of the camp, so Leslie went through the open window and approached the barbed wire.

In less than a couple of minutes he beckoned Gordon and me to follow and bring the "luggage" – which was practically all food stowed in three army rucksacks. All personal gear was abandoned and was used to build up dummies in the empty beds. When all three of us were through the window a last moment report came down the line that another guard was approaching the prisoners' quarters from the front. This guard was heard to call out in a loud voice for myself. A very quick-witted colleague engaged this guard in a conversation in pidgin German and explained that I was tired and had gone to sleep. As I strained my ears to listen to the manful efforts in the German language that were being made by my rescuer, I recognised the voice as that of Ginger Dobbs. He was a regular soldier with many years of service in foreign parts and as a result he scarcely ever spoke at length in plain English. Words of Hindustani or Arabic, picked up in India and Egypt, were incorporated in his dialogues. Building a small German vocabulary was something that Ginger had taken in his stride and as I listened intently in the darkness to what was going on round the corner I realised that Ginger was making his few words go a very long way. I did not see him again and so was not able to thank him for his good work. He had no doubt saved me on this occasion from being caught in the act of escaping which would have been frustrating and humiliating. I wanted at least a run for my money.

This little interlude provided the only tense moments for us during the break out. Up to that point none of us had suffered unduly from nerves, mainly because we had great confidence in our plans to get away. We had only experienced a kind of fidgetiness, rather like a family going away for a seaside holiday, wondering whether all the minor preparations were in order and waiting for the moment of departure.

The purpose of the guard's visit was to tell the band to stop playing and turn in. These instructions were passed on by my stand-in, and the band piped down quite literally and willingly – having done its job admirably.

Leslie had done brilliant work in cutting a neat tunnel through the double fencing and had cleared the intervening coils of wire. The general form was for each one to push his luggage through the tunnel ahead and follow it by crawling on his stomach, taking particular care not to catch his behind on any barbs above. Once through the wire a wide sweep was taken round the camp and we all three reached the railway embankment at which we were aiming at a point roughly a hundred yards from the front entrance to the camp. At that point the steady tramp of military boots was heard and a figure loomed out of the darkness, approaching the camp along the railway tine. We three "ex-prisoners" lay flat and motionless against the railway embankment. From a cautious peep at the figure passing by a few yards away it was seen to be the unmistakable outline of the Mother Hen. He was no doubt returning full of beer and cheer from the village and choosing the railway track as the surest and flattest route home. The dark cloudy night had saved us from discovery.

After these two narrow squeaks the next objective was a small patch of woodland further up the line, near the signal which so frequently halted the trains. Having made the spot it was just a question of keeping under cover until a train stopped. But no trains stopped that night and indeed very few passed by at all. Weeks and weeks of study of the pattern of the rail traffic, the destinations and the loads had shown that there was a good chance of getting a train with not more than a couple of hour's wait. Now something had gone very wrong.

There seemed to be no alternative to spending the whole of the next day hiding in the woods and waiting for night to come again. To abandon the vantage point and start walking was a great temptation, but it would have been a counsel of despair, because beyond that point we knew very little about the working of the railway. Nevertheless to remain stationary within actual sight of the camp from which the break had been made, and eating some of our precious food, was frustrating.

No guards came looking for us, probably because the Commandant did not expect us to be hiding so close to the camp. It was a gamble that paid off.

At long last darkness came again and with it a coal train, which halted. The three of us scrambled hastily across the ditch at the track side and over the signal wires.

It is quite a high climb from ground level into a coal truck and in the darkness it was no easy clamber over axle boxes and brake rods, but Gordon made it in a few seconds and acted as a human crane from above for Leslie and myself. Once aboard the truck the three of us concealed our silhouettes as best we could, by crouching down in the space between the side of the truck and the sloping pile of coal.

It so happened that this load was of unusually large lumps of coal, so it was a fairly simple matter to shift some in order to improve our positions. Very soon the train was off and although this was not the ideal form of travel, the rhythmic beat of the wheels over the rail joints was an exhilarating sound. The plan was working; this was a moment where our hopes were being fulfilled. In a few hours the train could be expected to leave German territory and be in northern Italy and from there we could plan again. At least it would be a useful section of the journey westwards completed.

Such were our thoughts as the train clattered along covering precious miles in the general direction of Switzerland. But it was not to be. Our train stopped at the railway junction of Villach. That was not surprising, but then, after a brief halt, to our dismay it began to move backwards into sidings which to our considerable astonishment were brightly floodlit. We realised immediately that luck had so ordained things that this particular train was the occasional one which replenished the coal bunker at the Villach depot. Our chances had been about fifty-to-one-against, but it had come up and wrecked our plan.

Under the glare of the floodlighting we crouched down in the truck for a hasty conference and decided that, after leaping out of the truck, a dash should be made across the open ground of the depot and into the darkness on the northern side of the town. We should have started in the opposite direction, but we could see that there was far too much town to the south of the depot for us to cross without discovery. Nobody was about in the floodlit area, but should any odd civilian have challenged us, Gordon would have dealt summarily with him.

Once we got clear of Villach we hoped that by bearing in a south-westerly direction we should again pick up the main railway line leading westwards and also the River Drave which, in its general line, ran parallel to the rail. Either would serve as a guide for our general direction, with the railway, we hoped, providing a chance of further transport. Alternatively, the river provided a hiding place on its wooded banks during the day.

In fact we performed this emergency deployment without too much trouble, picking up the railway again in the fitful moonlight and for the remainder of that night we kept up a steady trudge along the track. Before dawn broke we found a little copse which reached down almost to the water's edge of the River Drave, as a place to hide and sleep. Dried leaves provided a comfortable bed on which to lie; the leafy trees provided complete concealment from any chance passer-by on the river. Looking out from the shade of the trees into the outside sunlight, we could readily spot anyone approaching. Just after dawn we were afforded some amusement by the sight of an angler on the river bank who although blissfully unaware of being observed was in fact almost within arm's length of us. We spent a reasonably comfortable day, resting and gossiping about our prospects.

As soon as it was fully dark we set off again. The whole night was again taken up with dogged walking, always with the hope of boarding a stationary goods train. With a double line working on this route we knew there was little chance of one being held up. At one spot the nature of the terrain forced us from the little tracks we were using, on to a road, but the completeness of the black-out gave a reasonable margin of safety and we even exchanged the odd greeting in German with some chance passer-by.

All this peace, with some little progress, was infusing a feeling of security into us, but we had a nasty shock when suddenly a searchlight swept the road and lingered for a moment with all three of us caught in its glare. What was the reason for the searchlight at this spot? Suddenly we realised that we were in the outskirts of the town of Spittal where there was another large prisoner-of-war camp. The searchlight, its beam now stationary, was being operated from one of the camp watch-towers. Had our British Army uniforms been spotted by the searchlight operator? Would the next item be an order to halt, or a warning shot, or a shot with no warning? With breathless whispered consultations we decided to walk calmly on and to our surprise nothing happened. It was with considerable relief that we walked out of the searchlight beam and immersed ourselves in the darkness once again.

The valleys of Austria are dotted with numerous barns, serving as stores for agricultural tools and machinery on the ground floors, and the lofts for storing hay. The lofts were entered by separate doors high up under the gables, and normally reached by ladder. They provided ideal, comfortable and reasonably safe resting quarters for the daylight hours, infinitely preferable in all respects to the woods. The climb up to the hayloft door without the ladder, which was always locked away on the ground floor, was apt to be rather tricky.

The following night just as the three of us were preparing to leave such a barn, a mixed goods train halted at a nearby signal and although it was not yet completely dark we decided on a mad scramble to try and get aboard. We aimed for the middle of the train between the engine crew and a possible guard at the rear, but by the time we had chased frantically across the intervening ground the train had begun to move. When we got near, it had gathered sufficient speed to prevent us climbing aboard. We had narrowly missed a good opportunity for a useful lift westwards.

So our nights were spent in determined trudging. But with rations getting low, and still a very long way from our objective, our optimism began to dwindle, especially after one night when progress was nearly nil due to a colossal thunderstorm. This storm was an impressive spectacle, the vivid lightning of many hues and patterns suddenly illuminating long stretches of mountain and valley. Thunder crashes echoed and re-echoed in the narrow gorges. Between the flashes the darkness was intense and every momentary glaring illumination had to be used to try to espy a barn for shelter. But before one was found the rain felt in torrents. Travelling light, as we were, without coats and with practically all our luggage space taken up with food, we were soon drenched to the skin and floundering in open country.

We continued on, practically without any vision, except that provided by the sudden flashes. Water ran down our faces in little rivulets, and down our spines. I do not know how I looked, but the occasional flashes revealed my companions in a very sorry plight. Leslie looked rather like a man standing under a powerful spray shower. The weight of water cascading over him was so great that his hair lay quite flat and covered part of his face while Gordon, with jutting jaw and determined as ever, reminded me of a powerful swimmer battling to win a race in very rough water. Breathing had become a struggle for all of us. Again and again we would approach a dark shape in the hope that it was a barn, but the lightning would reveal nothing, or perhaps a tree.

One of the problems of the journey had been the supply of drinking water and I, being very dry, in a moment of folly filled my water-bottle from some gushing water in the darkness. I took a few hefty swigs and after a very short period was vomiting badly. The vomiting was weakening and meant also a serious loss of valuable calories.

At length a barn was found and Gordon managed to climb up the very slippery lower doors and so reach the hay loft. The climb proved a little too much for me in my weakened state, but Gordon, reaching down, caught me by the battledress collar with one colossal hand and hauled me into the loft. There all three of us stripped our clothes off and buried ourselves deep in the hay to keep warm. We were truly thankful to be out of the deluge.

With morale slightly dented but determined to make up for lost time we set off on the following night before it was really dark. After about half an hour of steady marching and lost in thought, we were suddenly startled by a bellowed: "Halt!" in German.

Two figures sprang out from behind a bush just ahead, a torch flashed and we found ourselves looking at very close quarters down the barrel of a submachine gun. We were also aware of being covered from one side by a double-barrelled shot-gun and not being out for suicide – this was obviously the end of the trail. Without any evasion, we answered the questions from the figure on the other end of the machine-gun, a well-armed, uniformed member of the Field Gendarmerie. I admitted that we were escaping British prisoners-of-war. On hearing this our two captors, the other fellow being a kind of local auxiliary police, moved cautiously round to our rear while keeping us covered. They ordered us to march and after a long trail up a mountain path we were locked in the outbuildings of a stone quarry and kept under guard for the night. That was the end of our freedom.

Surveying our situation, in that uncomfortable hut, we felt that at least we had had a good try, but that luck had been against us.

"I was on the point of taking a swipe at that bastard with the Mauser," said Gordon, meaning the chap from the Field Gendarmerie, "but the clever swine kept just out of range."

"I'm jolly glad you didn't, the gun was pointing at my solar plexus," I protested.

"Well, it's the end of our little canter, anyway" said Leslie with resignation. "It was a useful trial run, though."

Throughout the trip Gordon had been literally a tower of strength and a persistent optimist, although his optimism was based on an extremely shaky knowledge of geography. Unfamiliar with Europe and perhaps even distances generally, he was sometimes under the impression, after interminable hours of tramping, that we must have crossed some frontier or other. On one occasion when we passed a group of civilians conversing in the darkness he asked what language they were speaking! He probably hoped that I would say Italian.

Our week on the run had taken us to a spot near the village of Dellach, just over a third of the way to the Swiss border. The chances of a successful escape had always been slender indeed and even if the border had been reached the hope of crossing it, without local knowledge and in the face of frontier guards, possible mines and other barriers, was never very high. Our failure to get anywhere near the border was undoubtedly attributable to our had luck in not obtaining a longer lift on the train. But even though we failed it was worth the attempt for the sake of experience and it had made an exciting change.

VI *Gaolbirds*

So that was that! The following morning the three of us were collected from the quarry by an escort who was to conduct us back to the main prison camp at Wolfsberg. Before leaving I light-heartedly offered a cigarette to our captor from the Gendarmerie as a reward for his capture of us, and in the hope of making conversation. I would have liked to have found out how he knew where and when to lie in wait for us. Such information might have been very useful to other escapees, but both the offer and the conversation were turned down flat.

Back at Stalag XVIIIA, after being handed over by our escort, the next formality was to face a German Court Martial on the charge of attempted escape. The Court Martial consisted of two German officers, one of whom spoke fluent English, and a Warrant Officer. A number of routine questions were put to us regarding assistance we might have received in making our bid, and also what our goal was.

We were then asked if we knew what our punishment would be and when we greeted this with a casual "Oh, yes," the officer repeated in some astonishment "Oh, yes?" The sentence was normally three weeks in a prison cell, but he apparently did not know how well the prisoners had organised life for the inmates.

These cells, I should explain, were situated in a building in a wired-off compound within the camp precincts. At the entrance to this inner prison there was a kind of scoreboard which was used to indicate to an inspecting officer, and also to the relief gaolers, the number of inmates. The prison block was always full of "Englanders" (i.e. British and Anzacs) and there was often a list of those waiting to serve their sentence. There were also just a very few from other nationalities, probably French and Belgians, with perhaps the odd Russian or Serb. The French with a defeated and half-occupied homeland had no great incentive to try to escape, and the few who were in the cells were mostly there for other disciplinary offences.

The cells were about eight feet by six feet and were designed to accommodate two prisoners, with the least comfort possible. Apart from bare wooden bunk beds there was nothing at all in the cell. The barred window was boarded up on the outside at a slight angle from the perpendicular to permit a shaft of light and air to penetrate from the top. Once the inmates were in their cells the heavy doors were bolted, chained and padlocked. In each door there was a very small peep hole. Food consisted of a little dry bread and water for two days, with some awful cabbage soup with a single slice of bread every third day. No food or cigarettes were allowed to be taken into the cells and everyone was meticulously searched for such comforts before they went in.

Books, but no games, were permitted. Cells were searched during the prisoners' quarter hour morning walk in the tiny compound. At nine p.m. three blankets were issued, the only items of bedding, and were taken away again at 5 am reveille – leaving only bare boards. At that time cells had to be swept and occasionally washed out.

Such were the rules, in theory. In practice we had devised ways and means of making the lot of their gaoled compatriots considerably better than it was supposed to be. The basis of this was the principle of "adoption". Each inmate in the cells would be adopted by somebody in the main compound outside – usually one of his friends if they were around. The "outsider" kept him supplied with food and cigarettes whenever possible. A few of the guards were either friendly, or susceptible to bribery and corruption, or both. They discreetly allowed a certain amount of outside supplies to come in when their superiors were not at hand. They benefited themselves from this smuggling, with for instance, for every forty cigarettes sent in, ten would go to the guard.

The Red Cross parcels of the inmates were drawn by those who had adopted them and hot meals were cooked and taken to the prison when possible. Sometimes these were brought to the cells by the guard himself who would then take back the empties thus leaving no evidence. Cigarettes had to be kept concealed on the person otherwise they would have been confiscated during morning searches. Matches, also disallowed of course, were another problem but a good solution to this had been worked out. In the camp there was a kind of canteen supplied by the Germans but the only item of any real use on sale were very large toilet-rolls. One of these would be unrolled and then re-rolled with odd matches inserted every few winds with the ignition papers stripped from match-boxes inserted near the end. This system never failed.

Not all the guards were co-operative, of course, so the possibility of having hostile guards on duty for prolonged periods had been taken into account. Such periods were covered by a carefully pre-arranged plan for making contact. It worked in this way: the man in the cell would go to the lavatory at an agreed time. The procedure for this was to hammer on the cell door with the fists whereupon the gaoler at the end of the corridor would call out "Number?" The cell number would be called back and the appropriate door would then be unlocked. Once in the lavatory at the end of the corridor, the gaoled one would keep a close watch on the open fanlight high up under the ceiling, and if all went well a crude wire basket would slowly and quietly appear in view. This was on the end of a long pole being manipulated by the friend outside. In it there would be a dixie probably containing something like hot fried meat, mashed potatoes and peas; all of which had to be hurriedly consumed on the spot and the empty dixies replaced in the basket.

Success of such operations depended largely on having synchronised watches but in a military establishment such as a prisoner-of-war camp where things run strictly to schedule this was not too difficult.

Due to after effects from the sickness in the rain, I spent a short spell in the camp hospital with pleurisy and my prison sentence was deferred. As a cell companion when I did go in, I had a New

Zealander who was something of an old lag, having done a number of spells in prison. He had acquired an extraordinary technique of being able to sleep, or at least doze, for about eighteen hours out of the twenty-four. When he did wake up he would often remove his boot, take out a partly-smoked cigarette which had been tucked inside his sock under the arch of his foot and then, after lighting up, take a couple of lusty drags. After this preliminary, he would be ready for some conversation or reading.

I was magnificently looked after during my spell by an old friend, Hector Smith, an Australian infantry sergeant, who, on one occasion at five am on a Sunday morning, actually had the nerve to go right into my cell during cleaning up time and in breathless haste pull a wrapped cold treacle sponge pudding from inside his shirt and dash away again before any unfriendly guards spotted him! Hector had taken advantage of the milling throng when blankets were being handed in and cell doors were open. Cold treacle pudding is not everybody's idea of good fare early on a Sunday morning, but to the very hungry it can taste like wedding cake.

Hector was a fruit farmer from Melbourne, and like all the Australians I had ever met, a volunteer and a splendid type. Less rugged and not as heavily built as the average Australian he was nevertheless a strong leader. He once confided to me that he was a bit sore about not being awarded the Military Medal at Tobruk when it was first captured. He said he led the chaps through the barbed wire in his sector but the medal went to someone who followed him.

One of his failings was a rooted belief in his ability to sing. The Australians of course have produced some of the world's outstanding musical artists but the prowess of the Australian rank and file, in my experience, is even below that of United Kingdom community singing. It seemed that the German, Italian and Slav minorities in Australia had not yet been able to pass on their national talent in this direction.

In Steindorf, Hector had in fact been Camp Leader for a spell and had tried to organise "musicals". Occasionally these had been put on as evening entertainment in the mess room with Hector singing the leading notes in a flat baritone. One could recognise the songs from the words only, as Hector's efforts to strike the melody fell very wide of the mark.

He also tried very manfully at Steindorf to organise ad hoc Christian worship on Sundays without Bible, prayer book or hymn book. Inevitably he would try to lead his little "congregation" in hymn singing. I remember on one occasion, during the singing of "0 God our Help in Ages Past", even Hector was prepared to spare the Lord the ordeal of hearing the whole hymn by singing only the first two verses and then the last which of course begins "Time like an ever-rolling stream..." But Hector's memory failed this once when he said, "All right, chaps, we'll now sing the last verse, 'Time marches on!'"

However, time marched on very slowly in a cell with nothing to look at but bare walls. Apart from conversation with one's fellow sufferer, reading was the only distraction. However, even reading was made rather difficult when one day someone outside began nailing up the chinks in the boards over the window and sealing up the knot holes. They had afforded valuable shafts of daylight to assist reading vision. After much peering and focussing I spied the culprit, in the unmistakable uniform of a Frenchman.

In spite of all the hostility that I, and others, could convey in deficient schoolboy-abusive French, he went on with his job. Of course he was acting under German instructions, but any one of us in similar circumstances would have seen the Germans damned and have gone inside ourselves before robbing fellow prisoners of their scraps of precious daylight.

From time to time, the peephole in the cell doors was used by the more conscientious of the German staff to see what the prisoners were up to. One particular warrant officer was in the habit of tip-toeing up and down the corridor in order to catch somebody unawares. Sometimes in the cell one became aware of an unblinking eye looking through the peephole. For one Australian docker in the cell next to mine this sort of thing was too much. One day Sam laid patiently in wait determined that the eye would get an eyeful. When he knew that the super snooper was on duty he stood to one side of the peephole and awaited a suitable opportunity – to be signalled to Sam by his companion. When the eye was firmly implanted in the hole, Sam closed right in and spat. Inevitably there followed a furious jangle as the door was unbolted and unchained and the enraged German demanded to know what Sam meant by his action. Sam explained rather illogically, and with affected diffidence, that he suffered badly from bronchitis.

Sam was also a heavy smoker and one day after he had smoked a large number of cigarettes and the atmosphere in his little cell was like London on a foggy night, he received a surprise visit from the patrolling gaoler. When the indignant gaoler demanded an explanation, Sam laconically remarked in broken German that there was a bonfire outside and the smoke was drifting into his cell. In the ensuing search, he lost his few remaining cigarettes.

Although three weeks is but a short sentence it is a very tedious experience to be confined for that time in a bare cell. The hours tick by very slowly and I sought relief by alternately reading every book of P.G. Wodehouse in the scanty library and by studying commercial and technical German which was to prove very useful in later times. By good team work and ingenuity we so managed things that all gaolbirds emerged at the end of their stretch little the worse physically and with morale still high. This puzzled our captors no little!

It really was remarkable that the ordinary soldier of British stock never contemplated the possibility of defeat for his side. Hitler once said, probably for once with some truth, that "the nation's poorest son is also her truest one". This was remarkably accurate as far as the British and Commonwealth troops were concerned but it must be admitted that this blind faith was sometimes pinned on false foundations. For instance some believed that we would win "because we had the money", and again because "the Germans had no good generals". There was always the hangover from the early British propaganda about the Germans running out of oil. Anyway, without bothering about the logic of the matter, "we just knew" that eventually we should win. The consequences of losing a war against the Nazis were too horrible for contemplation.

VII *A More Interesting Life*

Figure 10: Inmates at the punishment camp at the paper factory. Oakes is
3rd from the left, front row.

At the camp to which I was sent, accommodation was provided for
the fifty or so prisoners-of-war in a very old, one-storey house,
situated just within the extensive grounds of the factory. The house
was also inhabited by rats and bugs that made our nights very

uncomfortable. As expected, the place was surrounded by a high barbed wire fence, but in addition there was an electrified fence as an extra deterrent to anyone who had ideas of escape. Along the full length of the back of the house was a small stream which actually washed its walls in places. All windows were barred and interwoven with barbed wire as well. The ratio of guards to prisoners-of-war was around one to six. So at least we could console ourselves by feeling that we were keeping quite a number of the enemy uselessly employed.

As a further precaution against any attempt to escape, all prisoners were required to hand in their trousers and boots at about eight pm. Thereafter they were obliged to walk around looking rather odd, or retire early to bed! The procedure of handing these items in, to be locked up in a separate room, was supervised by the Commandant's deputy, but nevertheless there was always the spare pair of "strides" hidden away for anyone who wanted to make a serious attempt at an escape and there were many who did.

We were engaged on shift work in the factory, including nights, and naturally those so employed were allowed to retain their trousers and boots. Once in the factory men were split up on various jobs and put under the charge of certain trusted Austrian workmen who were responsible for our custody and conduct. The military guards only escorted the outside working parties and patrolled the factory grounds.

All the United Kingdom, Australian and New Zealand internees had tried their hand at escaping, several more than once, and there were lots of tales exchanged. There was the lightly built, blond young Englishman who used to make his attempts dressed as a girl and was once recaptured whilst shaving in a wood. Two others had managed to buy Hitler Youth uniforms on the black market for their attempt, while others went in French Army uniforms, carrying a hay fork over the shoulder, just as the unguarded French farm worker prisoners did. In all they were an extremely lively and enterprising community and gave the Germans some awful headaches.

Life in the camp was considerably influenced by the presence of women working in the factory. Personal appearances, and manners, tended to slip in an all male environment, but seeing women every day was no doubt responsible for a little more attention being paid and improvement was quite noticeable. There were both Austrian and Russian women at work and it was strictly forbidden for us to have anything to do with any of them. The Austrian women and girls, robbed of the best of their menfolk by this stage of the war, were quite pleased to have us around and to progress from friendly to intimate terms when occasion and subterfuge permitted. This was simply human nature at work, and war and politics counted for nothing. In 1942, these simple, kind-hearted and lively women bore no hard feelings against us whatsoever – but that was before the massive air attacks on their country began.

The Russian girls were all just under or over the age of twenty. Very few were of the usual square, dumpy peasant type. Many of them were, unmistakably, quite well bred and well educated, yet they had become part of Hitler's slave labour force. Uprooted from their homes and families or what little was left of them, Russian women were transported to various parts of Germany and German-occupied territory to do whatever work was allotted to them. Many were nurses, schoolteachers or clerical workers but all were compelled to do manual work.

Life in Stalin's Russia was probably not all that much better, with another dictatorship every bit as cruel as Hitler's – but, when all was said and done, Russia was home and it was all that they had ever known. Then the Germans had come and smashed it all up and herded them into slave camps in distant lands. The Nazis did them a terrible wrong in committing them to such a life, without future or hope.

Possessed of a natural gaiety, gifted in song and dance, the Russian girls at the paper factory deserved something better from life than slavery but in spite of their fate, their morale was remarkably high. And their morals too. Rather unlike their Austrian counterparts, and considering their unfortunate plight, probably very few, if any, of the male prisoners would have tried to seduce them. The Russian girls seemed determined in any case to keep relations with boyfriends at a highly respectable level and even some of the accepted innocent acts of intimacy – like hugging – were barred!

Yet one way or another quite a bit of lovemaking did go on in the factory. The black-out and the many nooks and crannies of the sprawling factory afforded plenty of opportunities for lovers to meet. There always came that time on any shift when the Austrian worker in charge of his prisoner would knock off for a hunk of brown bread and bacon fat – during which time his charge would vanish, to meet his girlfriend at some pre-arranged spot.

We sought to help the Russian girls in practical ways, not merely because they were allies in the war, although that may have contributed to the feeling of sympathy which prevailed. But they were also fellow humans, and in trouble. We were now always in receipt of a weekly Red Cross food parcel, plus cigarettes and clothing, and in addition families and United Kingdom employers were able to send extra cigarettes and clothing, but no food.

Hence most of our real needs in the matters of both food and clothing were amply satisfied and as a result many knitted khaki items were handed on to the Russian girls, who unravelled them, dyed the wool, and knitted themselves additional clothes to wear. Also food was left out in various pre-arranged hiding places in the factory grounds for them to collect, and there were numerous personal gifts.

Although there were not very well off themselves, the Austrian women too were generous in passing on what clothing they could spare to the Russians. Footwear constituted a particularly difficult problem, due to the general and acute shortage of leather.

Like the Red Army prisoners who had earlier been helped in a small way by the British and Anzacs, the Russian girls were puzzled but grateful for whatever they received. It was rare indeed for any of them to resort to cadging, or to take the gifts offered to them for granted. Sometimes they would seek some means, however humble, to show their gratitude.

Amongst the Russian soldiers back in Stalag XVIIIA, there had been numerous skilled craftsmen who produced a variety of small pieces of artistry. They were happy to give their art as gifts to the British helpers. As Christmas 1941 approached, there was one quite unforgettable event in Stalag XVIIIA. Just before dusk one afternoon a whole crowd of Russians, now partly restored in health, assembled quietly at the barbed wire fence separating us and Russians. For some minutes, nobody knew why they were there and then suddenly it became apparent: the Russians began to sing for us.

Military songs and Russian and Ukrainian folk songs were sung with all that wonderful harmony, zest and temperament that the Red Army knows so well. The sight of this host of faces, singing lustily in the gathering gloom, breath steaming in the frosty air against a fading background of snow-covered mountains, made one forget the harsh realities of that life. "Music hath charms…" and it knows no frontiers and here was a tribute, a gesture of esteem for our help to them, that for many of us listening could not have been surpassed. Music is the form of art which reaches me more than any other and I derive the most from it when listening in solitude. On this occasion I moved away to a spot where I could watch and listen to this huge choir without disturbance. I was thankful, too, that the Germans did not wreck this moving scene. In Nazi terminology of the day this had been a case of sub-human Russians singing to the lackeys of the Jewish Plutocrats of Wall Street.

The Russian girls had little or no opportunity to sing in the factory and their acknowledgements took a different and sometimes rather embarrassing form. Partly because they had no other means of expression, but partly because it was a natural habit to them anyway, they made posies and garlands of flowers which they sought to present to we male prisoners whenever opportunity permitted. Sometimes this happened when a whole column of prisoners were being marched under armed escort. The girls would stand at the side of the road and hand over the flowers, either surreptitiously when the guard was not looking, or openly if they thought the guard was not a "terror". The British/Australasian male is perhaps not seen at his best when receiving a floral tribute, and often there were scarlet faces and deep embarrassment. But we knew what they were trying to express, and I am glad to say that in spite of the embarrassment they were never rebuffed.

The Russians, on the whole, seemed quite perplexed by our relative wellbeing. The food, cigarettes, chocolate and the new clothing from the Red Cross, were hardly in accordance with what the communist propaganda had led them to expect of decaying capitalism. Those who had swallowed Nazi propaganda were flabbergasted too. The

Russian girls were not slow to notice that the Austrian women were, relatively speaking, better and more stylishly dressed than anyone they had seen before. Western sophistication, although not strong in this rural part of Austria, had begun to make an impression and perhaps caused comparisons to be drawn.

A sure sign of the depth of this impression was the fact that the Russian girls set out to copy wherever they could. A large proportion of the little money they earned was spent at the local hairdressers, trying the hair styles of that era. These haircutting excursions were about the limit of the distance they were allowed to move.

The only physical recreation of any kind that we were able to enjoy in this camp was the odd game of football in the summer months. These were held on the local village pitch, but this of course only provided sport for the twenty-two players. So when it was learned that an Austrian colonel was to visit the camp it was decided to ask him to permit escorted walks on Sundays. Our excuse was that most of us worked in the unhealthy atmosphere of a factory and within the limits of the very small camp compound had no space for physical exercise.

The Colonel proved to be an amenable character, and a reasonably amiable one, and after listening to the request, ordered that forthwith we should have a walk on Sunday afternoons, provided that guards were available to escort them.

Our first walk was a great success. Girlfriends were alerted and turned up at carefully pre-arranged spots. Those without girls, and those whose girlfriends were unable to make it, had made arrangements with a farmer who worked part-time in the factory to call on him for a boozy afternoon session. The best guards – meaning the most friendly ones – had volunteered for duty and they joined in the drinking, knowing full well that on such an occasion nobody would attempt to escape. A meeting point was arranged for the various groups, along the route of the march back to camp.

Personally, I had spent the afternoon with Olga, a Ukrainian girl who back home was a hospital sister until the Germans had commandeered her. Twenty years of age, she was slender of figure and with rather delicate features for her nationality. She was vivacious but with a marked Slav tendency to switch at a disconcerting speed from laughter to tears and back again. Unlike some her colleagues, she had no hesitation in taking the risk of surreptitiously meeting an Englishman for the afternoon. The penalty for being caught would probably have been a few weeks in prison for both of us.

Dressed in an old red silk dress given her by some Austrian woman and with a recent hair-do, she looked semi-groomed and attractive except for her old broken-down shoes. However, with her quick wit and reasonably fluent German, she was good company. It was, however, very difficult with her, as with all the other Russians, to find out what was in her mind about her present situation in a slave labour camp, and how she viewed her future if she ever got back to her own country. All such questions received very short and noncommittal answers. One could not escape the feeling, sometimes, that if the choice lay between staying in Austria or returning to Stalin's Russia in her mind she was between the "devil and the deep blue sea. She wrote on the back of the card, "To my dear Grev" Olga. 14.11.43

Figure 11: Two of the Russian girls – Olga is on the right.

Indeed if the Germans had not been so savage and cruel in their treatment of the Russians and had instead played the role of liberator, they might well have won widespread support from both the civilian population and large sections of the Red Army. As it was, many thousands of Russians rallied to the German cause under their own Marshal Vlassov.

I must admit that politics was not the subject one chose to discuss at any length during a short and furtive meeting with a girl friend. We were concealed in a thick shady copse, commanding a splendid view of the Austrian mountains and valleys. We could also see the mountain path for some distance, so the approach of any stranger would have given us time to retreat to greater safety deeper in the woods. The sun shone brightly on that hot, cloudless day and no passer-by disturbed us. No sound was heard but the rush of a nearby waterfall, and it was good to see Olga smile.

Many were the friendships which grew up between men and women, through meetings in the paper factory. Most were probably only of a passing fancy or simply of delightful convenience to both partners. But not all. It is perhaps one of the great pitfalls of life that not many men, however hazardous or complicated the probable consequences, can resist a strong attraction to a woman whom they like and see frequently. Do what he may the attraction persists and it then becomes a question of whether he will pursue his desires in various ways or let them smoulder, and perhaps finally wither and die.

A few of the affairs at the paper factory certainly did lead to predictable complications and I was kept busy translating the two-way traffic in letters. From them I gathered that there was the beginning of a local Anglo-Austrian community. What happened to those relationships after the war, I have no idea. It is, of course, largely the sex urge in man that makes him the odd mixture of virtue that he is.

I often wondered for instance about Inge and Geoffrey, a charming and well-matched couple. She was Austrian, with black hair and slightly dusky complexion. She was very attractive, and normally she had a wistful expression on her face. It would lighten into a radiant smile and her dark brown eyes would flash in animation, when her temperamental nature was stimulated in conversation. She worked as a secretary in one of the Directors' offices. Geoffrey was an Australian from Sydney where he had worked as a bank clerk. Fair and of slim build, erudite and witty, he had an endless fund of conversation and would never let the company he was in subside into a state of silent apathy which came easily in prison life.

One very ardent relationship led to dramatic repercussions within the camp itself. The man concerned was a New Zealander, a farmer back home, who had volunteered like so very many Kiwis for military service, and had left his family to manage the farm as best they could. He was the kind of person who, whatever job he tackled, did so with energy and thoroughness by force of habit. It was a habit which he could not break and in the eyes of one or two fellow prisoners he obtained the odious reputation of being a too-conscientious worker for the German economy!

His relationship with an attractive Austrian plus the fact that he had a Germanic name, Herman, earned for him the exceptional animosity of one young Australian.

After one Sunday walk the Australian, Frank, returned slightly stimulated by alcohol stated that he was going to "sort out that German bastard, Herman," and challenged him to a fight. Frank was 23, over six foot and muscular. Herman was 34, much shorter in height but of sturdy build. It was the mistaken belief of some that the disparity in builds would lead Herman to reject the challenge. Frank was insistent and the reluctant Herman, protesting that such a performance was foolish and settled nothing, agreed to meet Frank on his terms.

The ensuing fight was properly arranged in one of the rooms, with a referee, timekeeper, seconds and all the doings. Frank demanded that the fight should be bare fisted and Herman, calm and still protesting that he disliked the whole business, agreed. Boxing gloves were in fact available from the Red Cross Sport kit if they had been asked for. A remarkably high proportion of all ranks in the British and Commonwealth armies were reasonably proficient with their fists and the fight that followed, judged purely from the technical side was of a quite high standard.

The simple Austrian sentry on patrol outside, probably never having seen boxing in his life, gazed in awe at the two powerfully built men, stripped to the waist and out to inflict heavy damage on one another. The guard made a feeble attempt to interfere but was told abruptly, as it was an internal affair, to mind his own business. After the usual skirmishing in the first round when the opponents were measuring up one another the fight livened up and Frank sought to gain a quick and decisive victory. However, Herman played a waiting game and parried and dodged the dangerous blows, while picking his moments skilfully and landing some telling body punches that left their marks.

Early in the fourth round he dropped Frank to the floor with a right cross to the jaw. After Frank had been "counted out", Herman walked quietly, head high, from the room.

Whatever Frank lacked in judgement he certainly made up for in blind courage for as soon as he had gathered his wits and his breath he demanded that the fight should go on again. Very reluctantly, perhaps because all along he had not underestimated his own fighting skill, Herman prepared to fight again.

In the second bout, it looked for a few moments that Frank was gaining the initiative and that sheer weight and stamina might gain him victory. It seemed that the effects of the alcohol were wearing off, but after tucking away a few damaging blows for a couple of rounds, Herman's better punching began to tell. Again he knocked out the young Australian and this time it really was for keeps.

This incident took place at the end of the second Sunday walking excursion and on the following Sunday there was another which, as it happened, was to prove the walk to end all walks.

A number of replacements had arrived in the camp to take the place of those whose punishment period had expired and the few who had escaped. Amongst the newcomers was the nucleus of a very hard drinking school, who saw in the Sunday outing an opportunity to make up for a lot of lost time. Accordingly, in the course of that afternoon, large quantities of potent apple cider were consumed. It was with great difficulty that the guards mustered all the prisoners for what was to be an epic march back to camp on a route which led through the main street of the nearby village. When the unsteady column was finally rounded up, it lurched and swayed down the mountain path to the main road, the now anxious and angry guards pleading for order and discipline.

The Australian element was in particularly uproarious form and there was little prospect of anyone establishing any authority over them. As the whole company came on to the main road, several of them were staggering an uneven course at intermittent pace. Somebody thought it a good idea to launch into song and the camp comedian, John Hughes, sought out a stave and placed himself as drum major at the head of the column. He gave a quite remarkable performance, even though his catching was at times a little unsure. As the camp came into view several hundred yards away the singing reached fever pitch, with a song, one verse of which ran as follows:

We are the boys from way down under Marching to victory.
We're not afraid of Hitler's thunder,

We'll put the bastard where he should be.

Suddenly it was realised that there were a number of figures standing at the entrance to the camp and on coming closer they were discerned as the Camp Commandant and the local District Commander who was evidently on a surprise visit attended by two of his staff. Their gaze was fixed on the approaching spectacle with no trace of amusement in their gaze – they gave just a cold, stony, inscrutable look.

The happy band was quite undeterred by this frigid reception and to crown it all the "drum major" called for an "eyes left" in passing the German officers. The camp spokesman and I were promptly called to the Commandant's office for the inevitable blast, the net result of which was – no more walks.

Soon after that incident a new Commandant was posted to the camp and immediately upon arrival announced that, unless discipline and work improved, escapes ceased and general standards improved, he was going to introduce an all-round tough policy towards the prisoners. It was pointed out to him that a tough policy would not succeed but he was an obstinate type and it was soon evident that a trial of strength was about to begin.

Life in a prison camp can be unbearably depressing especially when one has no idea when liberation will come, and in 1942 the end of the war seemed to us still a very long way off, as indeed it was! There were some who were reasonably content to settle down to a lethargic existence both mentally and physically, spending their spare time simply lazing around. Fortunately at this particular camp, amongst those with more lively and imaginative minds, there were a gifted few who were able to create humour where there was none, gaiety where there was boredom, and to stimulate interest where dreary monotony abounded.

Mention has already been made of John Hughes who, when he so desired, could turn the dullest moment into a riot of fun. Lively minds rebel against the oppression of acute boredom and frustration in an infinite variety of ways, some of them perhaps a little strange. The best will either invent, or clutch at, some situation and wrench from it something humorous or dramatic.

One example of this was Hughes' antics within the factory, usually in company with some of his like-minded friends. On one occasion he began whirling an imaginary ring around his forefinger to build up centrifugal force and then with a concentrated effort, accompanied by tense facial expressions, launched the "ring" high into the roof of the factory. Watching all the while in utter amazement were the Austrian workers. At the same time a friend further away watched the roof, intently following the flight of the imaginary ring and then anxiously and with hurried, panicky movements positioned himself in order to catch "it" on his forefinger. It was a variation of the performing flea.

Hughes was short and dark with a bushy moustache, a Scot and an engineer and in the course of his work sometimes handled an oxygen cylinder on a two wheeled carriage. One day this apparatus became his imaginary field gun and he went through all the paraphernalia of sighting his gun, taking the range, barking orders, loading and firing "shells" at his friends. Catching the spirit they countered with "small arms" fire from a trench, their "rifles" being the handles of the shovels they were using. The Austrians on this occasion saw the point and thought it all great fun.

A superb mimic and a quite talented actor, Hughes also had the extraordinary gift of imitating a foreign language. He produced with deceptive likeness the sounds and cadence of the language, without perhaps knowing a real word of it. One day a little group of Frenchmen, employed as outside labour at the factory, were conversing among themselves near one of the outbuildings when Hughes suddenly burst upon them. To them he was a complete stranger, and with excited gestures and the most animated facial expressions and shoulder shrugs began laying down the law in no uncertain way in rapid fire gibberish French. It sounded like French, but there was not a French word in it! To the Gallic ear it must have been something like our experience at British railway stations when loud-speaker announcements are so distorted that it is impossible to make out what is being said. Taken by surprise the French looked at Hughes at first dumbfounded, then frowning and goggling, and then looked questioningly at one another. Before they could rumble him, Hughes strode away with an expression of mock indignation. It was all over in seconds, and everyone who had seen it felt all the better for it.

Many pranks were played against the guards at that camp, especially against those who were backing the Commandant in his tough policy. The get tough policy caused one rumpus after another, and probably prompted an increased number of escapes. One amusing trick was played after the first snow had fallen in October. On outside patrol, guards carried their rifles with bayonet fixed slung over the right shoulder and held firm so that the bayonet pointed to the sky just behind the head and so beyond the range of vision. One morning when standing around in the compound somebody engaged the guard in some innocuous conversation while friends gathered about him in a group. While the conversation was in progress one of the conspirators very stealthily placed a snowball on the point of the bayonet and that having been done the conversation was broken off and the group dispersed. The pay off came, of course, when the Commandant loomed on the scene and spied one of his sentries plodding around oblivious to the fact that a snowball was perched, nicely frozen, on the top of his bayonet. The chap then got a rocket for presenting such a ridiculous and unmilitary spectacle.

At eight o'clock each evening when boots and trousers had to be surrendered, the Commandant's deputy came around to give the order. He was not a particularly disagreeable man and did not cause any special resentment, but he had a very marked stutter. His was the kind that gets stuck on initial letters and in this respect the order in German for the handing in of boots and trousers contained more than a fair share of pitfalls for one with such an impediment. The order was, "Alle Hosen and Schuhe heraus!"

As he went around repeating this command an echo could often be heard in the distance, with the same hesitations and hold ups: it would be Hughes giving the same order in another room.

But for one of the particularly hated guards Hughes had a special surprise packet in store. All night long guards would have to patrol the barbed wire and electrified fencing which ran the length of the narrow compound. The guard had to pass an open barred window which was situated very close to Hughes' bed. One fairly dark and chilly night when the special enemy was on his monotonous beat Hughes lay in wait, unseen, beside the window. It was approaching midnight and there was no sound from anywhere, save the tramp of the sentries' boots. The darkness was relieved only by a little starlight. Backwards and forwards, backwards and forwards, the guard plodded, apparently lost in thought, no doubt trying to forget about his miserable sentry duty, and envying the prisoners supposedly asleep in peace in the warm. Then, as his head came level with the barred window, Hughes let rip with a fiendish, piercing, graveyard cackle that even startled Hughes' room-mates who were expecting it. As far as could be ascertained in the gloom the guard seemed to take off sideways and, of course, by the time he had recovered his wits and his breath, everybody was back in bed and seemingly asleep. There was nothing he could do because there was no question of anyone owning up, and to report the matter to the Commandant would only have invited scorn.

Peaceful coexistence with the prisoners was the only answer, if a guard hoped for a reasonably comfortable life. There was one more guard to be sorted out. He was a nasty type and tried to play the old game of running with the hare and hunting with the hounds. He would tell us what a good chap he was and how we could trust him – then sneak-report any misdeeds to the Commandant. When it was his turn to make the final count of the prisoners at night he poked his nose into everything and in addition he was a shocking cadger for all those things that we had from parcels, but were in short supply in Germany – such as chocolate and good pipe tobacco.

One such night when he became a pestering nuisance in the room furthest from the Commandant's it was decided to take action. The door was closed and two prisoners stood guard over it. The guard's hat was removed and a merry game started of tossing it from one to another. Every time the victim lunged to get his hat it was flung to another player and the guard given a hefty shove into the centre of the room. As he was unarmed while on this indoor duty there was little he could do to retaliate. He had to endure this infuriating prank in a spluttering rage until he had been goaded long enough and was allowed to go – with a warning about his future behaviour. He had little chance of telling the Commandant since the latter expected his guards to exert authority and to command respect.

There was however one very serious incident which occurred just about this time. Most of the prisoners were employed round the clock, on shift work in the factory and about five fifteen one morning one Australian was roused by the guard to go on the six am to two pm shift. The Australian's name was Twist, so inevitably he was known as Olly. The guard had made a mistake on this occasion, as Olly was working another shift and was entitled to continue sleeping. After trying to explain the situation, Olly settled down to sleep again.

The guard persisted with his mistake and roused Olly again whereupon the latter became angry and told the guard to go away – not his actual words – and disappeared under the blankets again. Not to be denied the guard fetched some cold water and made the fatal mistake of pulling back the blankets and pouring a little over Olly's head. For the more rugged Australian there comes a time in any dispute when words are of no further use and action takes over. Such a moment had arrived for Olly. He sprang out of bed and with a savage blow sent the guard sprawling backwards, across a bench and with a yell and a clatter, he disappeared under a table.

This pandemonium brought the Commandant from his office next door and sizing up the situation quite inappropriately drew his pistol. Olly was no doubt a little flushed by his quick victory and possibly was still looking belligerent, but without a moment's hesitation or consideration the Commandant pointed his pistol at Olly and pressed the trigger two or three times. But no shot was fired.

It transpired that the Commandant had acquired for himself a rather fancy Italian revolver, with a faulty mechanism. He was using German ammunition and the combination of these factors certainly saved Olly's life. Enraged by the situation the Commandant bellowed abuse at Olly and then ordered him to be kept under close arrest until the arrival of the local Commanding Officer. He was summoned by telephone and when he arrived a long talk with the Commandant ensued, of which only the merest scraps could be picked up by eavesdropping.

The upshot was that Olly was escorted back to Stalag XVIIIA to face a court-martial, at which he was found guilty on the charge of indiscipline and assault. He was sentenced to several years imprisonment at the notorious fortress prison at Torgau in Poland. However, Olly did not serve one day of that sentence. On the day that he was supposed to have been transported to Torgau, with collusion from an Austrian officer he "disappeared". Just before departure, he was left alone for a few moments at the Administration Office. Seizing his chance he made off into the great throng of prisoners outside in the compound and until the end of the war lived "in smoke". His hide-out was never found and the prisoners' infiltration of the German Administration was so effective that he was able to receive his mail and enjoy most other amenities. For much of the time he mixed freely with other prisoners, safe because we always seemed to get adequate warning of impending searches.

To return to the working camp at the paper factory – the cold-blooded brute who had made the attempt on a defenceless man's life had the effrontery to ask Hughes, of all people, to do what he could to repair his defective revolver. Hughes firmly declined. As a reprisal, it was decided to try and steal the revolver in an unguarded moment and to throw it into the river. The Commandant would no doubt have been forced to report the loss and may have faced a charge of negligence. Alas, no unguarded moment arose.

There were however some further dramatic events which finally led to the Commandant being posted elsewhere. A most audacious escape was made by two prisoners one evening when they made a quick dash through the camp gate. While it was being held open by a guard to allow a party of prisoners back into the camp on their return from work, they ran through. Shots were fired at the two as they disappeared into the night but neither was hit. Escaping without food or belongings, so as not to be impeded by any gear, they fled to a prearranged spot in the hills. There they were supplied through the collaboration of friends in the camp and the Austrian communists from the factory.

There were several communists in the factory and they proved in word and deed to be very steadfast friends to us, a combination of Austrian kindness backed by a firm anti-Fascist party discipline. Being regular listeners to the BBC, they would give us the war news every day. In later years we learned with sorrow that several of them had lost their lives in concentration camps.

At the other end of the social scale there was a local Austrian nobleman and his family who were very pro-Allies in every respect. I had many a conversation with this gentleman and he frequently enquired about my welfare and that of my friends. He had some charming old-fashioned notions about the British way of life that could not be shaken and I think he sympathised with me in being denied the facilities for whistling "Tipperary" in a hot bath every night before dressing for dinner.

An event which caused a tremendous stir at the time was the attempt to set fire to one of the paper warehouses where a large store was kept. Although paper was not a key product in the German war economy, the quantity produced at this particular factory was very considerable when related to total output. The loss of a fully stocked warehouse would have had some repercussions in other sectors of the "war machine". A carefully prepared and timed attempt to get a blaze going was made by an Australian, supplied from outside the camp with the materials. The blaze started one evening as arranged; but just as it was getting a hold an Austrian worker, who by sheer coincidence and extremely bad luck had chosen that moment to smoke a cigarette outside the factory door, noticed the flames. He promptly raised the alarm and the fire was out in a very short time indeed.

A meticulous and thorough enquiry began, involving the Gestapo who rightly suspected arson. They made a very careful examination at the scene of the fire and then pounced on our camp. Every tin, bottle and container of every description was scrupulously examined and accompanied by vociferous protests from the prisoners, the place was turned upside down. The Gestapo were the people who terrorised so much of German-occupied Europe, who forced entry into people's homes in the early hours of the morning and hauled them away to an uncertain but terrible fate. It was strange to observe those dreaded men being told in a very emphatic way, to "knock it off" or "clear off" and that by prisoners!

Of course they did not clear off, but although they continued with their job, they clearly felt their authority was being challenged. They found nothing incriminating at all, but rather than let the matter drop altogether on purely circumstantial evidence, charged a prisoner with causing the fire.

It so happened that at the moment the fire started this unfortunate person was the only man reported absent from his place of work. He was in fact having a slightly longer meeting than usual with his girlfriend, but was an entirely innocent party as far as the fire was concerned. That was his bad luck. He had to appear before a court martial which, though unable to pin the crime on him decisively, probably felt unable to acquit him after Gestapo participation in the case. So as a kind of compromise they passed a light sentence of imprisonment. This was of course rather distressing to the real culprit, but obviously there could be no confession.

Such were the variety of ways in which different types of people let off steam. We all lived in a small, strange and restricted world but as Milton said "The Mind is its own place and in itself can make a Heav'n of Hell, a Hell of Heav'n".

A quite different incident that primarily concerned me led to an astonishing series of consequences. By that time many prisoners had acquired some knowledge of the German language and could make themselves understood to a small extent. But this knowledge was obtained from working daily alongside Austrian workers, with the result that the vocabulary and pronunciation were based on very broad Carinthian and Styrian dialects which sometimes are not understandable to North Germans. I once listened in fascination as one prisoner, quite unabashed, addressed himself to a senior German officer in the broad Carinthian dialect and to make matters worse, he used the "familiar" and disrespectful form of address.

As the only fluent German-speaker in our happy band, it fell to me to collect news regarding the military and political situation from two factory workers, who were probably communists, who listened to foreign broadcasts. Although I have referred to the British & Commonwealth POWs as a 'happy band' there were times when the deprivations and restrictions on our lives evoked sudden bouts of bad temper under neurotic pressures. I was no exception in these circumstances and one day, to my own surprise, turned upon a group of 3 or 4 workers having a short morning break. Working up a good head of steam I flayed them, as I put it, for working for Hitler, voting for Hitler and fighting for Hitler, and pointed out that the Germans were getting bombed day and night and the sooner the RAF came over to sort out the Austrians the better.

There were no interruptions during my spontaneous outburst and at the end I surveyed without remorse a group of very dejected-looking faces. They reminded me of a spaniel's face when suddenly deprived of an evening walk. Hindsight revealed that in one sense I had addressed the wrong people but in another sense the right people. I was not to realise at the time what consequences would spring from my tirade.

VIII *Military Intelligence*

The following day, Mr Zeller', a senior member of the management of the factory called me aside, and told me that he had heard about my outburst on the day before. At this I expected the worst, having already been warned back in 1941, by a Camp Commandant for saying disparaging things to civilians in regard to the Nazis. On that occasion I had been threatened that imprisonment in Rawa Ruska Camp in Poland would probably follow, if any further cases were reported. Walls had ears in Nazi Germany (Rawa Ruska was a strict regime camp).

But to my surprise Zeller[3] stated, with very little introductory formality, that he was one of the leaders of a local group in the Austrian Resistance. He wished to know whether he could count on me and my friends for their support in the days to come. Not knowing at that time that there was an effective Austrian Resistance, this came as a surprise to me, though a rather stimulating one.

Zeller told me that his group in the valley was about three hundred strong; with arms hidden in caches in the mountains. Their broad intention was to harass the German rear when the Allies reached the

---

[3] Zeller is not his real name.

Brenner Pass. Zeller had always been a slightly unknown quantity to us. A few said he was a reliable anti-Nazi but I had never made up my own mind. All we knew about him for certain was that he was at the factory, that he lived in a house at the nearby village and his family was reported to consist of a wife and two children. He was a dark, rather handsome, slimly built fellow of perhaps 35 with a Hitler type moustache that had always put me off a bit.

Always correct in his behaviour and in a restrained way, even slightly friendly in his attitude towards the prisoners, Zeller had never before revealed his inner thoughts. Now, having broken the ice, he was speaking as if his anti-Nazi stand was something which I should take for granted, and which did not require explanation. His political leanings I assumed to be those of a Social Democrat or some similar moderate Left Wing movement. He pointed out, several times with some emphasis, that the only people he wanted to join him were those who would be "prepared to go through thick and thin" when the time came. Playing for time, I said that Zeller's proposition was quite unexpected (which indeed it was) and that I would have to do some thinking before making any comment.

Left alone with this surprise packet I pondered on a number of problems. Zeller's statement gave me a very different outlook on the countryside and its natives. But how reliable was Zeller? Was his organisation really effective? Did it even exist? I was pretty sure about this last, but who was I, anyway, to make any kind of decision regarding my fellow prisoners' participation in his activities? To give each man in the camp the option of lending his support to a desperately risky adventure would have meant canvassing each one in turn. That would clearly have been letting too many people into the secret. I was of course holding a very, very hot potato and desperately wanted to share it with someone.

Guerilla warfare is of course a specialised thing for which proper training and equipment and a thorough knowledge of the terrain are first requirements. None of us in this little camp had any of these, but clearly Zeller's proposition and his plans should not receive a bucket of cold water from us. For my part, I must confess that I felt the prospect of being engaged in a hazardous behindthe-lines action against a powerful and ruthless enemy, a chilling one. To decline participation however, if the opportunity arose, would have been shaming. So I committed myself in spirit to the scheme and tried to derive comfort from the thought that in irregular hit and run actions one's morale and skill is likely to improve with practice. But most of all I found relief in the thought that the vast, deserted tracts of thickly wooded, hilly country in the area would provide ample hiding places for an armed force. It would have been a most difficult job for the Germans to find the manpower to comb the whole countryside for small gangs of saboteurs. There were lonely stretches of railway lines and roads that were quite easy to attack in the hours of darkness.

There was no point, I felt, in consulting anybody back in the camp. It was not that I distrusted my friends there, but I felt that this important matter was not one for a local decision, but concerned the highest British military authority available. That meant a visit to someone in the main camp, Stalag XVIIIA, which after all was only a few miles away.

I cast around for someone to consult there and decided without much hesitation that a trusted man, Lawrence by name, seemed to know a good deal prominent personality in the camp and took a leading part in many activities there, especially those concerned with the theatre. I knew him well enough to to have seemed that he was highly intelligent in a quite unobtrusive way. I knew that he took a leading part in escape activities and I had a hunch that he was probably involved in deeper and even more secret activities. He was one of that rather unusual type who could talk brilliantly about anything he chose, but usually prefer to say nothing at all. About his own interests, likes and dislikes, hopes and fears, none of us ever learned a thing!

The problem of how to get to see Lawrence was eventually solved by a visit to the dentist. Despite having perfectly sound teeth, I put in a request for an examination, requiring a visit to Stalag XVIIIA.

On arrival I "reported sick", skipped through the dental inspection quickly, and leaving others to be attended to, hastened off to find Lawrence. I found him without difficulty, and as I had half-expected, he listened to my story as if it were some everyday business, asked a few penetrating questions, and then gave his decisions. He told me to press Zeller for more details about the variety and extent of his organisation's stock of arms and ammunition, types of weapons and to find out where the local Landeschutz (Home Defence) Battalion kept its armoury. Lawrence seemed rather more interested in turning Zeller into a source of military intelligence, and he gave me testing questions to put to him:

(1) To find out the location of the battle HQ of the German Army on the Southern Front in Italy and (2) the identity of the German C-in-C of the fighting forces there and (3) the location of Hitler?

We would keep his interest because of our supplementary questions, with Lawrence calculating that in the period before guerrilla war started (if it ever did), Zeller might be steered towards supplying military intelligence.

Nothing, of course, was written down during this interview and before leaving, I asked Lawrence to approve an alternative go-between messenger. I would have difficulty making regular contact with Lawrence, and suggested Ted Lamb, Australian camp leader and our spokesman at the factory. His duties took him occasionally into the Stalag and I suggested he would be acceptable as a courier to bring in any reports. This was agreed to by Lawrence who knew Ted well; and so a small espionage network was in the making.

On my return to the factory I found a convenient moment to talk to Zeller about the matters discussed with Lawrence without of course mentioning the latter's name. I could see that our plan was a neat compromise but it did nothing to discourage Zeller's ideas for active resistance. In these exchanges Zeller generally inspired confidence and there seemed no reason to doubt that his information was given in good faith. Resolute, shrewd and quick witted, he evolved a method of conducting talks which gave the impression to any possible onlooker that he was issuing instructions regarding factory work, making the necessary gestures to lend effect. All his answers were short, precise and in clear German, but with the noise of machinery nearby there was no danger of our conversation being overheard. He took very readily to the idea of providing military information and said that he had some well-placed reliable friends who could be exploited to this end.

Within a week he had provided the name of the German C-in-C in Italy and the location of his battle HQ which, as it happened, was just over the Austrian border at Eichberg in the Dolomites. He also ascertained that it would remain there only until 30th September 1942, after which it was expected to move elsewhere but Zeller did not know the new location.

He also told me that Hitler was apparently visiting Zell am See in Austria, but he had no further details. These details were later given verbally to Ted Lamb who learnt them off by heart and conveyed them to Lawrence on his next visit. Lawrence did not press for further specific information, but told me that he would like me to make the fullest use of Zeller as a source of information.

Further discussions took place between myself and Zeller, whose interest had by now been well and truly stimulated. He was prepared to report on anything of military interest, passing on any information he could pick up by means of his contacts.

In my dealings with Zeller I was assisted by my pre-war interest in international military and political affairs. There were of course many fascinating characters on that stage, such men as Churchill, Hitler, Stalin, Mussolini, Allenbrooke and Rommel to mention but a few. When the mind is keenly interested in a subject the memory will do great work in storing information on it. I clutched at all there was to read about politicians' speeches, the relative military strengths and types of weapons and ships and aircraft and this background knowledge came in very useful in my conversations with Zeller.

Very early on in our association he gave me a short but factual account of the underground construction of a Herman Goering armament works in the valley of the Mur. On another occasion he even obtained some details of Hitler's visit to Austria, although it was of little practical value as there was little time to act. These items were fed back to Lawrence as swiftly as opportunity could be devised.

Perhaps Zeller's best effort was when he volunteered to spend part of his leave in making a reconnaissance, as far as local security would permit, of the Messerschmitt Aircraft works at Aspern near Vienna. I suggested that a cup of ersatz coffee at the nearest cafe might provide an opportunity for picking up a few more details either by overhearing conversations or by putting a few guarded questions. When he returned to give me his report he also told me the date when the aircraft production for the month would be assembled and tested on the ground. This information he had been able to glean from workers engaged there.

Zeller must have realised that in passing this information he was in fact giving details of a target which would invite heavy air bombing from the Allies. He showed no compunction in doing so and it was obvious that in his mind the struggle against National Socialism in Austria must be carried through without being squeamish. The fight would be to the bitter and bloody end, although that inevitably meant heavy Austrian casualties.

By joining Ted Lamb on a genuine administrative job concerning clothing at the Stalag, I was able to make the journey to Lawrence and give details of the aircraft works to Lawrence personally. He was deeply interested and said the information would reach British HQ in Italy within twenty-four hours. How this was done I did not know, and I knew better than to ask[2]. I suspected naturally that he had access to a secret radio transmitter. What one does not know one cannot betray. Lawrence produced a map from a hiding place and in my presence made a pin prick in the name Aspern. There is no doubt that of those of us involved, Lawrence had by far the most difficult and dangerous task, in sifting information which he received and passing it through.

It was some days later, in September 1943, on the very day that Zeller had reported the assembling and testing as taking place at the Messerschmitt works, that for the first time a serious air raid took place on Austria. The first American planes flew over close to the paper factory in the direction of Vienna and perhaps it was just coincidence, but perhaps not. I could not help feeling a tingle of excitement in possibly again playing some small part in the war out of which I had, officially, been cancelled. Until the liaison with Zeller I was able only to follow the war from second hand BBC bulletins passed on by Austrian friends who listened to them, or the biased German Press.

Whether in fact the aircraft works were bombed on that day I did not discover and it would have been foolish to pursue enquiries. Then, before further news became available the Germans decided to close down the prisoner of war camp at the paper factory.

To us this was a nuisance, and entirely unexpected. It seemed that the escapes, the fire, and the general record of disturbances at the camp must have forced the German Administration to the decision to close it down. As well as the fraternisation with friendly workers, there were also love affairs with women known to be going on, although nobody was ever caught. Zeller even found a foster father for an illegitimate Anglo-Austrian. The Germans decided to scatter the prisoners over other working camps, so as to dilute the strength of the troublemakers and this was done, giving us no warning whatever.

In many ways this was a disappointment and particularly as my link with Zeller was beginning to prosper and now it would be irretrievably broken. The camp had become quite a reasonable one after the Commandant who had tried to shoot Olly had been posted elsewhere. His place had been taken taken by a pure German who had been wounded on the Eastern Front. The new Commandant was Oscar Hey, whose home town was Trier. He left nobody in doubt that he believed until the very end in a German victory and had the greatest faith in Hitler's ability.

But he also believed in just and sympathetic treatment of POWs and not even after a couple had escaped did he become the least bit ruffled. Instead of angrily demanding the names of the missing, as his predecessor had, and making things tough for the remainder, he calmly checked his list, made his report to his superiors, and let it go at that. He recognised that it was the duty of a soldier taken prisoner to escape if he could and as a result of his general attitude life in the camp itself had achieved some sort of stability. The break-up of the camp also broke up many a friendship. We had been a congenial lot, and there were many new-found companions I was sorry to say good-bye to.

But there were no regrets whatever on leaving the living quarters themselves, where the rats and bugs at night had made life very trying at times. There were sad partings from girlfriends, some of them a real wrench. And as all the prisoners were marched under escort to the railway station early one morning in October 1943, most of the Russian girls stood at the side of the road to wave good-bye to their friends whom they were never to see again. As they waved some of them wept.

It was a pity that after a few months, during which Zeller had passed on some high level intelligence, the arrangement had to end. Although a married man with a family and very much aware of the terrible fate that would befall all of them if he were caught in his activities he took the risks willingly, in fact gladly. But I felt that he was a gifted conspirator and with my ready-made fairly regular access to Lawrence, the set-up had seemed as sound as could ever be expected.

I learned subsequently that Zeller and his merry men had gone into highly belligerent action later in the war, successfully knocking out a number of Waffen SS vehicles. This news was obtained from a letter which Zeller wrote to me after the war. As he did not mention any casualties in his group I assume that he had led some successful hit and run raids, probably during the hours of darkness.

IX   *The English Cup of Tea*

With four of my friends from the paper factory I was sent to a camp where prisoners were employed unloading coal trains at a railway siding. Unlike our previous residence this camp appeared to have settled down to a peaceful life. The allocated piece-work enabled the prisoners to finish their labours by lunch time and to indulge in sport in the afternoon. Everyone seemed to have made his little corner in the camp a homely spot. No criticism should be levelled at those who were content to "sit out" the war and make life as comfortable as possible, but for many this was too dull.

The first morning at work I discovered that the task allotted to me and a companion was to unload a coal truck which, from the consignment note, contained 26 tons of coal. Had the regular inmates of the camp not settled down to similar tasks as a matter of course, I would not have believed the job to be humanly possible. I had chosen the biggest and strongest of my friends to help, and I got into the truck with the large water hose to damp down the dust which was the normal procedure. The hose was in fact connected to a very powerful hydrant, and whether by accident or design somebody turned on the main cock to full strength and the force of the water made the nozzle almost leap out of my grasp. A colossal jet of water

135

hit the side of the truck and the splash-back promptly soaked me. For self preservation I immediately directed the water elsewhere and one of the people I hit was the guard – a genuine accident. Not a good start!

The two of us toiled all afternoon to unload the truck, whereas all the regulars had finished before lunch. We decided that this was not the life for us. All five of us from the paper factory decided to report sick after two or three days although there was not a genuine complaint amongst us.

When I joined the army, I was tall and slender. In the early, hungry days of captivity I had lost much weight and was consequently dubbed Atlas by some Australian friends. One said I looked like an undernourished greyhound. Now, thanks entirely to the Red Cross parcels I was, like most others, completely restored in health and strength. There now occurred a fortunate collusion between camp doctor and the Commandant, who wanted to retain the peaceful atmosphere of his camp. He did not want troublemakers from outside to disturb the situation, so when the five of us reported sick, each giving a lurid and fanciful story, we were all certified as unfit for work at the camp. Nothing could have been further from the truth.

At that camp there was no contact with civilians; there were no women, and the empty coal trucks went back to Silesia or the Ruhr which was no help for escapers. We became bored stiff. Thus our little group returned to Stalag XVIIIA with our certificates, hoping that the next posting might prove more favourable.

Figure 12: A Scottish act. Left: a camp poster. Bottom: cast include John "the burglar" third from left, with arms folded.

We found that life in the Stalag for the permanent staff and the "floaters", had improved considerably. The theatre drew its talent and technicians, the actors, singers, painters, script writers, designers, electricians, carpenters – and even a milliner – from the ten thousand British Commonwealth prisoners from Greece. Music was provided by a competent orchestra which had been formed by Bill Southworth of the London Symphony Orchestra, using instruments from the Red Cross. He had taken in his stride the adjustment from playing classical music to forming an orchestra to cope with stage musicals.

Sport was also flourishing and some football matches were even staged with the Russians, who used gear that was smuggled through the wire to them. They changed into their uniforms and slipped into our compound to play matches that were billed as "England v. The Hammers". The Hammers were not up to British Army standards and it was usually arranged to make the match a draw.

One everlasting problem hung over the prisoners – that of never having enough fuel to feed the stoves on which we did our cooking. All manner of means had to be adopted to make good this deficiency, with a heavy toll being taken of the predominantly wooden construction of the stables in which we were housed. Mangers, sundry panelling and fittings of various kinds had been sacrificed, much to the anger of the Germans. But there were other and more daring exploits.

At night, as well as guards in the watchtowers armed with machine-guns and equipped with searchlights, there were others who patrolled the great length of barbed wire fencing surrounding the huge compounds. Provided for those guards were a few striped wooden sentry boxes in which they could shelter from wind, rain and the intense frost in winter. One night, just after a guard had left his shelter and had started on his long weary trudge along the wire, a few enterprising prisoners silently carried the box away to their barracks. By the time the unhappy guard had returned to his box it was already providing the fuel for a brew up on a large scale.

This kind of activity compelled the Germans to introduce guards accompanied by Alsatian dogs inside our compound. As a result a few prisoners lost bits of their trousers.

On another occasion the Germans planned to build a new lavatory in the compound and this job was undertaken by a local Austrian builder. It was of course to be an all-wooden structure (timber being the local product), a large affair looking rather like the bottom storey of a pagoda. The builder, a naive little man, made his estimates regarding material and one afternoon brought in carloads of timber in preparation for work to begin the following day. When morning arrived the pile of timber had been very considerably reduced and thinking he had made some mistake the builder fetched more. But when the same thing happened again the light dawned and a guard was mounted to protect it from us marauders. When, at considerable cost in material, the lavatory was finished we began dismantling the superfluous parts of the construction and then, shortly afterwards, decided that we could dispense with the roof too.

One day the SD (Security Service of the Gestapo) swooped on our compound in force and began going through the place thoroughly. Among the areas which they searched with the greatest care were the lofts above our quarters, to which access was obtained by a long ladder leading to a trap door. They searched assiduously with torches for hours at a time, probably looking for transmitters, receivers, compasses, maps and so on. In one of the stables when three of the SD had disappeared into the darker reaches of the loft, the untended ladder was very quietly removed by a young Tasmanian. Aided by friends, it was taken to another building where it was chopped up in double quick time for the fire, providing one of the best brews of tea for many a day.

I went along to observe the reaction of the three SD men in the loft. After they had spent much time on a painstaking search their faces finally appeared in the aperture in the ceiling. After the first surprised blink they called out in German to the nearest prisoner below and asked where the ladder was. The prisoner at first pretended not to hear and then when the inevitable shouting started, looked up at the three red faces framed above, shrugging his shoulders to indicate that he did not understand German. Then he casually shuffled away. A well prepared act!

Eventually in response to their shouts the SD men were discovered by a guard, but this was not quite the end of the story. There was no

140

other suitable ladder in the camp and it was far too high to jump from the loft to the stone floor. There was no alternative but to send someone down to the town to get another ladder, entailing a lengthy wait for our three visitors in the loft.

Reprisals followed as a natural consequence. First of all a mass parade was ordered in the camp which was attended by everyone, of all nationalities. Interpreters were called forward from each nationality to hear a general lecture on law and order, for passing on to their respective contingents. Then dismissing all the other nationalities we British were told to stand fast. Then followed the mother and father of all lectures on discipline and obedience. It was pointed out that the war was not over and the Allies were not going to win it anyway. The Germans would instill discipline at any price. And so on. It was then demanded that the man responsible for stealing the ladder should take two paces forward and own up. The culprit did not own up and nobody would have wished him to do so under any circumstances. Thence followed a string of collective punishments, such as early lights out, a total ban on sport and recreation, and each announcement was greeted with a cheer from the incorrigible audience, with a spontaneity, baffling to the Germans. As on many other occasions I was convulsed with laughter, a state which renders an interpreter somewhat useless.

I remember too that as each restriction was bawled out in German by the Commandant, a bush whacking Aussie who could understand the gist of what was said would yell back: "Good on yer, sport!" It was

141

no wonder that some of our guards took a positive dislike to us – the more so as every tightening of discipline against us made extra work for them!

Later the Germans decided on what they thought to be a a masterstroke. They argued that it was the British and Anzac "Diziplinars", of whom there were always a fair number in the Stalag, who were the root cause of nearly all trouble and lack of discipline. Admittedly our unruly bunch were a bit awkward at times, even when so great a person as the impressive General Graf von der Schulenburg and retinue visited us. As he arrived at the camp for inspection, it was difficult to drive the prisoners on to parade. The German logic figured that if this bad influence was segregated, kept in a small separate compound of its own, under strict guard, they would be contained and tranquillity would reign throughout the camp.

Thereupon the construction of a new wooden barracks began in our compound and the building was surrounded by a high, double barbed wire fence. Eventually the day came when it was ready for occupation, a day for which the Diziplinars themselves had well prepared, as they had no desire to be fenced off from their friends. The accommodation consisted of a single wooden building in which there were rows of three-tier bunks with straw palliasses. The march-in took place later one afternoon and according to plan the first few prisoners went in carrying just a few belongings and unobserved, put a match to some of the straw palliasses. When they were sure that the flames had a hold they shouted "Fire!" and fled from the building. Outside the guards in panic called for the camp fire brigade not realising that this would help but little.

The Diziplinars, because of their low social standing, were required to do all the fatigues and odd, sometimes dirty, jobs about the camp. Amongst their odd jobs was the manning of the fire brigade, a duty which, being in the general interest of everyone, it was thought they would do conscientiously.

So they did, usually, but not this time. They dived frantically for the hose reels, moved swiftly into one another's way, became entangled with the hoses and generally put on a very fair imitation of a slapstick comedy act. When somebody did eventually stand with the nozzle at the ready before the blaze, only a little trickle of water was produced which fell gently to the ground.

Next morning the German "master plan" was a heap of smouldering ashes and the only regret I heard expressed, was that so much wood had burned and not a single cup of tea brewed. What comments were made about the incident on the German side we did not care to enquire.

X   *Klagenfurt and the Gestapo*

Figure 13: The Municipal Building in Klagenfurt, 1940s.

My next posting was to a large camp situated on the outskirts of Klagenfurt, housing several hundred prisoners. The overwhelming majority of prisoners in the various camps were those who had been taken in Greece and on Crete. Occasionally a few were to be found who had originally been captured by the Italians and then handed over to the Germans, or those who were seized from Italian camps when Italy changed sides in the war. Curiously, many of these asserted that the general treatment from the Germans was better than that encountered with the Italians, who all too often proved to be petty and spiteful as captors.

Klagenfurt is the provincial capital of Carinthia, a town dating from the sixteenth century, with many charming corners and a few of the inevitable "onion" spires. It is relatively low-lying and on one of the outskirts, surrounded by wooded hills, is the attractive lake known as the Woerthersee.

The camp itself consisted of wooden huts forming a square and the centre compound was used as a general recreation ground. It was in fact just large enough to stage a reasonable game of football in winter or cricket in summer. Also near the centre was another wooden building which was the communal wash room for people and clothes.

From this camp prisoners were sent out each day in parties to a variety of jobs. These included cutting ice blocks from the lake in winter for the breweries, general road repair work and the unloading of trucks at the railway sidings.

Some were employed at individual shops and some even worked in the stores at the local Waffen SS barracks. In these barracks, when occasionally left to their own devices, they were able to tune in the radio to Britain, or some station under Allied control, to get the latest war news. One old sweat of the British Regular Army used to add the most unpalatable things to the SS soup when he found it unattended and simmering in the kitchen. There were also rich pickings to be had by those who were not too worried by scruples. The Waffen SS, Hitler's picked fighting troops, enjoyed many privileges in the German Armed Forces and amongst these was a priority regarding alcohol. French wines, brandies and liqueurs, as well as the best of German produce, were in their stores. Naturally some of the prisoners helped themselves, concealing the bottles under their battle dress blouses when they returned to the camp at the end of the day.

This went well for a time but the game was up when some of them overdid it. They had a super party back in the camp and were later seen rolling around uproariously drunk. The SS Commanding Officer had the working party paraded before him, where they expected a proper blasting. In fact the Commanding Officer made a very human speech about the kind of things in life that he would miss if he were unfortunate enough to be taken prisoner. He said he could therefore understand those who had helped themselves, adding that one or two bottles would probably have been all right but they had overdone it and if it should happen again there would be punishments. And that, remarkably enough, was the end of the story. Life was full of surprises!

The camp was large enough for some well-organised sport, and various other kinds of recreational activities. At Christmas time the mess hall was used for a Christmas party with games and songs providing the main entertainment. The decorations were quite gay and someone had even procured some contraceptives which were blown up as makeshift balloons. In the summer of 1943 a miniature Empire Games was held in which England, Australia, New Zealand and Scotland and Wales competed as teams in all kinds of events ranging from athletics, football, darts, table-tennis, bridge to tennis. The tennis was played on quite a good improvised court, using Red Cross sports gear, and some high-class matches were seen between a few fairly high-ranking Australians and New Zealanders. Frank Woolmer an Australian, won the Tennis singles final and Australia won the entire " games" quite easily and by a handsome margin.

From the beginning of 1944 Allied air raids on Austria became more and more intense, as the British and American air bases moved northwards in Italy and more of that country came under Allied occupation. Almost every morning, the clear crisp atmosphere would reverberate as hundreds of four-engined American bombers flew from the south, often passing quite near to Klagenfurt. There were exceptional days when the bombing would be particularly severe with formations of bombers flying in all directions. Examples of the special days were Hitler's birthday, Easter Sunday and various Nazi anniversaries. Though these raids had a highly stimulating effect upon the prisoners, they certainly did not improve our relations either with our guards or with the civilians we met.

In my spare time I was supposed to be studying to become an accountant. I had gathered the necessary books from various sources but the Americans' activities rather frustrated my attempts to master such ponderous and involved subjects as mercantile law. I remember reading as far as page three of a massive volume on this last subject and then the throb of millions of American horsepower caused concentration to falter! Perhaps because they had a very real bearing on the war and the re-shaping of post-war Europe, I did find the economics easier to assimilate and concentrate on. My studies, including the technical and commercial German, were not altogether fruitless, as I returned to Germany after the war in the Foreign Service. I was not the only one spending part of our interminable "spare-time" in trying to prepare for the future. A number of students who filling the unforgiving minutes in studies to become engineers, solicitors and even doctors.

One very brilliant winter's day a large formation of 'planes was observed at a great height and appeared to be approaching Klagenfurt itself. The town had no air defences and conditions seemed ideal for the attackers. Their target turned out to be the training airfield at Annabichl on the outskirts of Klagenfurt, but on this particular raid the USAF missed the field altogether, but devastated the adjacent cemetery instead. We prisoners then had the unenviable task of putting the dead back to rest.

This large cemetery, with its sea of ornate crosses and gravestones had been turned topsy-turvy. Dead sinners and good people alike had been unceremoniously shaken up by high explosive.

"I think the poor old bastard in there will have been seasick," said Steve, a Sydney docker, nodding towards a coffin which was standing nearly head uppermost. "Get back to your harp, sport," he added as he tried to ease it back to the horizontal.

"I bet the Yanks will come back and make a fair dinkum job of the airfield," I commented.

A few days later the Americans, who were obviously fully aware of their miss, did come over again and this time made no mistake. Just after these attacks anti-aircraft batteries moved into position close to the prison camp. In casual conversation with the locals, I discovered that the batteries had come from Hamburg, where they had no doubt had plenty of practice. This was an interesting snippet of intelligence which I passed on to Lawrence at a later date.

One sunny Sunday afternoon, soon after the arrival of the guns more 'planes came towards Klagenfurt at a great height, the sun picking out the shapes of the bombers which glistened like a swarm of gilded insects against a pure blue sky. At first the formation seemed to be by-passing the town but then, with what seemed almost an afterthought, it turned towards the town and began losing height rapidly. Excitedly we began to count as they came lower. The German batteries opened fire at an intensive rate and almost at once got the range. The barrage was so accurate that the puffs of black smoke of the exploding shells were spot-on amongst some of the 'planes. But the Americans flew steadily on still losing height for the attack but not forsaking their neat formation. This was obviously going to be carpet bombing.

When the count of 'planes had reached over seventy of the four-engined bombers we sighted another wave approaching and decided it was time to turn away and duck. With no air-raid shelters the best the prisoners could do was to lie flat on the floor of their huts and hope for the best. The roar of hundreds of engines was tremendous, as the guns boomed and the huts trembled. Then above it all came the shattering noise like many express trains passing by at once, as the bombs all came down together. There was one devastating cataclysm of high explosive as the bombs fell into the township itself. The impact made the earth shudder and, with my head under my bed, I could see and still vividly remember, many thousands of particles of dust leaping up and down on the floor-boards in the rays of a clouded sunlight. Pictures, utensils and all kinds of odds and ends came clattering down on to the floor.

A moment later everyone leapt up and went to the opposite window to see the aircraft which had passed over, but at that moment the second wave attacked and we went down again. This wave over, everyone went to look at the departing American bombers once more and to watch the agony of the three which had been hit and were on fire. With anxiety we counted the number of opening parachutes as those who could baled. Those who were knowledgeable on such matters could tell us roughly how many airmen had not made it and lost their lives.

Immediately after the raid all prisoners were mustered to go into the town to help in the rescue work. On the way we were met with whistles and boos from the citizens and even a few stones were thrown. Although the first effect of these positive counterblows by the Allied Air Forces was stimulating and was thought at the time to be hastening greatly the final victory, the spectacle of so many civilians, including the old, the sick, and women and children, blown to pieces or desperately wounded, was a cruel one to behold. It hardly seemed relevant to the main purpose of the war. On looking back, I still doubt if it was. The planned killing of so many civilians will certainly not constitute a page of glory in the history of the Western Powers.

During the evening alerts, when nervous tension began to build up, Summers, the camp's very accomplished pianist, would disappear into the mess room, which also served as a concert hall, to play on the grand piano. With only moon and stars for illumination he would transport himself, and other fortunate ones, with fine renderings of Beethoven, Bach and others of the great composers. How fortunate Summers and his like were in having in their hands an art which could transform and transcend whatever surroundings they found themselves in!

In January 1944 I had a remarkable piece of luck. It was in relation to my intelligence work, which was unknown to, and, I think,

151

unsuspected by anyone in Klagenfurt at that time. Several of the prisoners at their place of work came into contact with Austrian women and naturally relationships sprang up. Very often, due to the presence of guards or perhaps other civilians who could not be trusted, there would be few opportunities for conversation. As a substitute for what could not be said, letters were written and furtively exchanged by both partners.

Although, the majority of the prisoners by this time had acquired something of a working knowledge of spoken German, usually overlaid with a shockingly thick Styrian or Carinthian accent, reading and translating a letter was quite often beyond them. When I arrived at this camp, I was a stranger to most of my fellow prisoners, but as a German speaker I was soon roped in to help with this kind of two-way correspondence.

On one particular occasion I was translating a letter for a friend named George who was on intimate terms with an Austrian woman in the town at the place where he worked. At the end of the letter was a paragraph about the Germans making all haste to get as much oil as possible out of Rumania. She wrote that she had spoken with a railway employee who was handling consignment notes for many thousands of tons of oil. This was being sent by rail to Austria, where it was being stored in a grotto in the Arlberg.

I asked George, who was a shop assistant in civilian life, why his girlfriend had written such a thing. He suggested that some Austrian woman somehow fondly imagined that the prisoners could somehow get in touch with their military headquarters. She probably thought that in passing this information to an Englishman she was doing something against the Nazis and so helping her conscience.

I was sure that the woman had not imagined the story about the oil, and in light of the military situation at the time it was plausible enough. With the Russians pushing the Germans steadily back and the latter having to reckon with the possible loss of Rumanian oil, they needed to stockpile supplies. I told George to encourage further information of a similar nature but his friend should not tell anyone else. I also insisted that nothing should be put into writing and if it was, that it should be on a separate piece of paper for easy concealment or destruction. The letter containing the news about Rumanian oil was hastily burned. The basic details were easy enough to retain in the memory and by a happy chance I was able to pass it to Lawrence a few days later, together with the news and location of the anti-aircraft batteries in Klagenfurt. When I handed the information over I had a comfortable "well that's that" feeling! But subsequent events made me uneasy – to say the least.

Some weeks later there was a sudden swoop on the camp by men of the SD (the security service of the Gestapo). All huts were searched by about ten of these professional snoopers. As an example of their thoroughness, my mattress was ripped open, and the anti-bugs brown paper and pin up pictures glued on the walls were ripped down. Prisoners were then paraded and thoroughly searched, some being forced to remove their boots and socks. All the while the SD were given the usual lusty abuse which, of course, was to no avail, though it did relieve our feelings a little.

As a private soldier just over 20 years of age I could hardly have rated as a prime suspect in the minds of the Gestapo but as a fluent German speaker I might have been. Even though three Gestapo officials had given me rather individual attention when searching my hut I did not feel that they could pin anything on me and my morale at the time was bolstered by two other factors. One was that I stood nearly a head and shoulders above the three officials and also felt that intellectually they were not very bright. Secondly, I was flanked by burly Australians and New Zealanders who besides making encouraging noises in my support were roundly abusing my interrogators. I am convinced that had the Gestapo started any of their customary rough stuff on me they, even though they were armed, they would have received some mighty blows from powerful Commonwealth fists.

Whenever the Australians felt provoked into abusing their captors their tirades were always richly interspersed with four letter words. The Germans, of course, soon became aware of this and when officiating as an interpreter in a fracas between Australian and German I was sometimes asked by the latter, "What does 'fucking German bastard' mean?" It was impossible for them to comprehend how this much overworked word could in turn be a verb of motion, a destination to go to, an injunction to depart and an attribute adjective applicable to anything under the sun!

Nothing of any significance was found anywhere in the camp, so that was one up to us!

According to camp rumour, and it was probably true, the Germans were becoming very worried about leakage of information out of Austria. Whether it was true or not, in my capacity as a collector of intelligence I took great care never to have anything in the least incriminating on my person or among my belongings. Though it was an uneasy period for those with love letters to conceal, I did not feel myself to be in very much danger.

Regarding the leakage of information from Austria, however, an event occurred which gave me further cause to wonder. Less than a mile from the camp, unknown to me and most other prisoners, there was a very small factory making aircraft wingtips. The factory was actually a large farmhouse with outbuildings which had been converted for its new purpose, and precision production machinery installed. The Americans accurately bombed this minute sector of the German aircraft industry, demonstrating that even this little "factory" and its location was known to them. A party of prisoners was drafted to clear up the mess, myself amongst them, but when I discovered the nature of the job, I maintained that it constituted war work and refused to do anything. I was alone in this stand but the guards did not seem willing to make a great issue of it and left me alone. I spent the morning walking round, far and wide, counting the bomb craters. They had used sixty-four bombs just to destroy this little place. No wonder war is expensive.

A month or two later considerable speculation arose in the camp regarding evening visits by a middle aged German in civilian clothes. He spoke excellent English and was courteous and casual in his approach as he strolled around the grounds on peaceful summer evenings. Sometimes he would enter one of the huts and begin informal conversations. These visits took place at irregular intervals and I soon noticed that when he arrived at the main gate of the Camp, where he had to show his identity papers to the sentry on gate duty, the sentry on inspecting them stiffened, handed them back and gave an extraordinarily smart salute. This led to the assumption that the man must have been of considerable importance with some military or police background.

He was probably either the SD in plain clothes, or a member of the Abwehr (German Military Intelligence). In his conversations he sometimes mentioned that he would like to meet any prisoner who could speak German. I decided that if the visitor desired a chummy chat, with some hidden motive, it would be a good thing to give him a miss. I contrived to be at the opposite end of the compound to the German whenever he was around.

The Commandant and his staff seemed to have extraordinarily little knowledge of the personal particulars and qualifications of the hundreds of the prisoners under their charge. The result was that they seemed quite unable to help in any preliminary filtering for the "visitors". This did not quite fit into the orthodox belief of the organised German mind, but perhaps there were too many Austrians involved!

We conjectured whether they were recruiting prisoners for the British "Bulldog" SS Unit of the German Army to fight in Russia. The visits petered out and we heard no more about the matter.

From all we could hear at this time the war was going well. We could see very little, but hear plenty for, at this period, we were fairly well served with BBC news bulletins. Somebody had access to a radio and as a result we had a news bulletin read out in each hut every evening. The Allied campaign in Italy was progressing rather slowly, in face of stubborn German resistance (the Italians themselves having packed it in ages ago), and all the while the Russians were keeping up their relentless pressure on the colossal Eastern Front.

On one of the working sites there was a German foreman known to us as Big Hans. A very big man, and an ex-soldier, he, like so many of his countrymen, had a fearful premonition of what was coming to his country from the East. In any discussion on the war he would invariably cast an anxious eye over his shoulder eastwards and talk of the fateful struggle going on in that direction. And perhaps there was a gnawing conscience which prompted thoughts of Russian retribution. The Russians were expected to exact revenge for their own terrible sufferings by the Axis forces in the mightiest clash of arms the world had ever known. But of course the East has always been a hypnotic magnet and a nightmare to the Germans.

All through the spring and early summer we had been kept agog in expectation of the grand invasion of the West European mainland by the Western Allies.

Sweepstakes were run as to where and when it would take place. I took every opportunity to read the military commentary in the Nazi Party newspaper, the *Volkischer Beobachter*. If one was prepared to read between the lines a little as well as along them it, rather surprisingly, often gave a fairly objective appraisal of the military situation. In addition, when the invasion started the German radio bulletins were rather more forthcoming than the BBC was allowed to be.

Major blows by the Allies, such as the invasions of Sicily and Italy, called for some celebration in the camp and to provide the "wherewithal" a little secret distilling came into play.

One of my best friends in Klagenfurt was Mike Collins; born of English parents in New Zealand, he had spent a large part of his life in Australia and Europe. He had joined the New Zealand Infantry at over thirty years of age, and with only one eye at that! He had managed to fiddle his enlistment, maintaining that a man needed only one good eye to shoot with! A fairly prosperous man in the wine and spirits business in civilian life, he always said "Give me any form of vegetable matter and I will produce alcohol for you". Accordingly, packets of prunes from Red Cross parcels were "laid down" in water to ferment, with the help of yeast which was procured on the black market. When the fermentation period was over the liquid was distilled by a carefully made contraption and of course in great secrecy. The distilling itself was a long and wearying process, catching drips from the condensed steam arising from the boiling of the liquid while someone had to watch for guards.

Extra efforts had been made for the occasion of the Normandy invasion, and Collins produced some extra potent "Jungle juice" or "Giggle Water". On the day of the landing, there was an evening celebration where several of the company in the hut in which Mike Collins and I lived, worked up into rollicking form. As the night wore on and in supremely high spirits an uproarious rendering was given of the German song "We're marching against England!" This song, like "Panzers advance in North Africa", had been strictly forbidden in German ever since the Wehrmacht had gone into reverse gear and all hopes of an invasion of Britain had been abandoned. "We're marching against England" is a splendid song and I knew the words having heard it again and again and had taught it to my friends. Now the marching was to be the way.

At the height of our surging chorus, a dim shape appeared in the black-out, silhouetted against the bars of the open window of the hut. With no more ado Mike picked up half a cucumber from the table and hurled it at the intruding head and, in spite of the alcohol and only one eye, he appeared to be bang on target. It was the Camp Commandant. Uproar followed and guards were hurried in to restore order, and as a result, a few of those who had been celebrating spent three days in the camp cells. But the news we had been celebrating was worth it! As I had been one of the instigators of the occasion, I felt a little guilty that others were imprisoned but not me.

In July 1944, the camp leader, a rather small, quiet Australian named Stubbs, approached me with a surprising suggestion. Without revealing the source of his information, he said that he had learned that resistance groups in Yugoslavia were stepping up their efforts to liberate prison camps. It was known that General Mihailovic of the Royal Yugoslav Army had some bigger plans in mind to this end, and wished to have a German-speaking British/Australasian prisoner down at his HQ in Yugoslavia for discussions.

I was asked if I would be willing to go on this mission, though it was explained that so far only tentative arrangements were in hand. I was not sure why I had been selected for this approach. The Australian camp leader was an aloof person who kept very much in the background and knew me only by sight. I therefore assumed that I was earmarked as the only fluent German speaker in the camp and that a sound knowledge of the language was considered an essential for the job. Stubbs incidentally had a fair working knowledge of the language himself.

The rough idea was that I should escape from the camp at night, not in itself too difficult an undertaking, and thereafter I would be picked up by a courier, who would put me on a goods train, with a friendly train guard, bound for Yugoslavia. There, at a pre-arranged spot, contact would be established with one of Mihailovic's men. More precise details would be forthcoming later. I agreed to the scheme in principle but waited in vain for further news. It was presently learned that the British Government had more or less ceased to support General Mihailovic and was now backing Marshal Tito. This was probably why nothing more had been heard, but in any event I decided on the strength of this news that I would not go anyway. Becoming mixed up in any way with Yugoslav domestic squabbles might have had abrupt and unfortunate consequences. Having got so far, and with the war going so well, I was beginning to feel that after all there might be a future for me at home!

To us, the next momentous event was the German plot against Hitler's life. The news, and multitude of wild rumours surrounding it, spread at an amazing speed. The division between the German Army and Nazi Party had always been fairly apparent to me, and in my very small way I had often been able to exploit this for our benefit. I appealed to the inherent military chivalry of the German Army officers, while being hostile to any Nazi Party men that I met. It seemed to me that on the national and international plane, the situation presented by the plot would be utilised to the full. This would certainly be done by the British, to bring about Hitler's downfall. But the plot of course miscarried. The Nazi organisation regained its grip and the German Army, amongst other things, lost its military salute in exchange for that of the Nazi Party – just one clear and slightly comic demonstration of where the power really lay.

In August 1944 George's rather indiscreet lady-friend found she had another piece of information to report. Remembering that she should not put such information into a letter, she instead wrote the details on a separate piece of paper and tucked it into an envelope with the letter! The piece of paper gave the precise location of an alleged very large poison gas works' near Breslau (now a Polish city), some figures on the numbers of people employed there, and explained that the information had been obtained from an Austrian with anti-Nazi sympathies who had been on business in the Breslau area.[4]

Reading this note in privacy I realised that I was holding in my hands a ticket for a very hot seat indeed if it was discovered in my possession. After feverishly learning the details by heart I burnt it with a sigh of relief. I told George not to tell anyone about the letter and even though it seemed to be killing a goose which laid a very nice line in golden eggs, I resolved that this form of reporting must be stopped at once.

Every agent who gathers secret information is prone to think that his or her piece of information is all-important, and that no other person can gather similar, or better, information and that his HQ will be excited at receiving it! I was no exception to this general run and considered that I must do all in my power to get this news to Lawrence as soon as humanly possible. I argued to myself that with the war going badly, Hitler out of sheer spite and anger, of which he

---

[4] It was subsequently revealed that the factory near Breslau was manufacturing Sarin and Tarbun nerve gases and Hitler chose not to use them out of fear of Allied retaliatory chemical warfare.

had plenty, might well use poison gas in a last desperate fling. In defeat he might try to inflict the maximum in misery and destruction of human life, even on his own people.

I also believed that I must convey this information in detail to Lawrence personally and not through an intermediary. The great problem was how to get back to Stalag XVIIIA. I could not request to be sent back and reporting sick would not have helped either, since the camp at Klagenfurt had its own little hospital and local doctor. I was anyway, now restored to health and strength, thanks entirely to the Red Cross, and at over twelve stone I was too fit to feign illness. German doctors by now were always sharply on the look-out for malingerers.

There seemed only two possibilities of getting back to Stalag XVIIIA. One was to make an attempted escape, to be recaptured, and consequently be returned there for the inevitable court martial and prison sentence. The other possibility, the one I adopted, involved having someone who was a genuine invalid, report sick using my name. It was easy for a camp official to detach a name and number from one person and add it to another.

In the Klagenfurt camp there were one or two prisoners who had more or less permanent disabilities, such as anaemia or asthma. They could, if they had so wished, be returned to Stalag with a genuine medical certificate. For various reasons, including dislike of the restricted Stalag life, horror at the poor food, the desire to stay with special friends or girlfriends, these semi-invalids stayed put.

I therefore approached one such prisoner, a fellow suffering from anaemia, who in return for fifty cigarettes was prepared to report sick in my name and with my number, in order to get me the required ticket for Stalag. As a general rule neither the guards nor the Commandant knew one prisoner from another and the trick worked satisfactorily. There was of course the major problem of arriving back in the main camp, a picture of health, with a certificate from a local doctor testifying very much to the contrary. At no time would the prisoner, in such circumstances, have possession of the relevant medical papers as they were carried by the escorting guard. I knew that situated between me and the German Staff doctor in Stalag there would be an officiating Royal Army Medical Corps orderly, who was a friend of mine. He was a New Zealander named David Prendergast, who could be relied upon to destroy the false documents, and I would then become just another "floater" in the camp.

I had reached my decision to leave Klagenfurt after long deliberation, because it meant that I would be cutting myself off entirely from the source of information supplied by George's girl-friend. There would be no possibility of returning to Klagenfurt again. On the other hand, the flow of compromising letters to George was always liable to be intercepted, and if one containing information of military importance was picked up it could have meant shocking disaster all along the line.

However you looked at it, it was a very dangerous situation, and I reckoned it wise to "take my profit" and call a halt. In addition to the obvious risk of interception, be it accident or ill luck, there was another indirect, but very real risk. Local newspapers frequently published an odd paragraph about illicit love affairs in which "shameless German women" had "comforted the enemy". The penalty for such women was usually shorn heads and a long prison sentence and there was also severe punishment for the prisoner.[5] The Germans were continually on the watch against this fraternisation, and if they had got on the track of George's affair, who knows what else they might have discovered?

So very early one morning, six days after obtaining the news about the poison gas factory, I set off for Stalag XVIIIA. I could not help feeling slightly amused at the thought that the Germans were providing an armed escort to ensure that I got there safely with my information.

---

[5] The wording "shameless German women" is an indication of how Austria had been made part of the Greater Germany Reich and renamed "Ostmark".

XI *Lumberjacks*

Back in Stalag XVIIIA, I was successful in having the false medical certificate extracted and destroyed, in order to save an embarrassing interview with the Chief German Medical Officer. It was necessary however for me to produce a cover story for being there at all, and after consultation with a British Army doctor in the camp I joined the daily sick parade. My story was that I had imaginary internal symptoms which sounded convincing and were, I was told, difficult for any examining medical officer to disprove without prolonged tests. Thus I was left in peace for a few weeks.

I had, of course, been able to see Lawrence and make my report. He listened with keen interest, checked one or two details and that was that. I assumed the information would be quickly passed back by transmitter – where, how and by whom, I had no idea. Collaboration with Lawrence had always been stimulating. Completely self-assured and with a firm grip on his side of the intelligence business, he had always been content to let me manage my side in my own way, acting on my own judgement.

In order to avoid being sent out on working parties, many prisoners in Stalag XVIIIA went to extraordinary lengths to be certified unfit for work. By now, only the German Medical Officer's word was good enough for a prisoner to avoid work. Some told lurid stories about tropical or desert illnesses, knowing that the Germans were not familiar with these, sometimes succeeding – at least for quite a long time anyway. One Australian, Dusty Miller, by putting on the most fantastic acts, even convinced an International Commission, consisting of one British, one German and one Swedish doctor, that he was mad. He was certified insane and repatriated, but had to endure a number of rather painful injections in the process.

Others induced a variety of symptoms just before seeing the doctor. One trick was to swallow small pellets of soap to produce an irregular heartbeat, and another was to make the skin rough by rubbing it with something abrasive and then applying skin cream obtained from the German canteen. This produced a rash, which was known as "Egyptian eczema". A few even went as far as scalding themselves or producing self-inflicted wounds – anything to gain respite from the dreary long days of work.

By October 1944, like most others, I thought that the war would be over very soon. So I decided to try to fix a drafting to some working camp far away from any town. There I would spend the last few weeks of the war in rustic surroundings and comparative peace. By the time I left Klagenfurt the air-raids, day and night, were becoming really intense. It is a somewhat difficult business to keep the traditional stiff upper lip in face of attacks from your own side, particularly when you have no adequate shelter.

Because of the number of indispensable prisoners helping in its daily business, the German Administration of Stalag XVIIIA was "bent" and as a result a number of fiddles were possible. As luck would have it, and very good luck it was, I managed to get myself posted to a very small camp of twelve prisoners engaged on lumber-jacking high up in the hills of Styria near Graz. Away from any village, in a tiny community of three foresters' houses and a little saw-mill, it seemed a good spot from where we could watch the curtains come down on Hitler's Third Reich and the last dramatic acts of the war.

The timber camp was a prize for any POW. The tiny unit made military discipline virtually impossible, and relations with guards and civilians were correspondingly relaxed. My record was not good; attempting to escape, charged with occasionally being drunk and threatening, I was lucky to get such a good pitch in which to "sit out the remainder of the war and await the grande finale". We all felt sure in the autumn of 1944 that victory was just a matter of days or weeks and nobody thought of making plans for escapes. Sit back and relax was the general idea, but how mistaken we were!

We twelve prisoners were quartered in a log house with a commandant and a guard. The accommodation consisted of one large living room, with beds, a long table, forms, and a stove for burning sawdust. There was also a small kitchen, alive with cockroaches. To wash we had to use an open air water pump fed by the fast-flowing mountain stream which flowed nearby. In winter when the temperature was sometimes minus 10 degrees C and below, ablutions did not take long. One prisoner stayed at home all day to do the cooking and "housework" while the others were engaged as lumberjacks on the surrounding wooded hills, which belonged, somewhat incongruously, to the Order of the Knights of Malta.

I arrived at this haven escorted by a guard from Stalag XVIIIA, once again a stranger in what was obviously a well established camp or rather, in this case, a household. On being introduced to the twelve I felt that I was being summed up critically to see whether I would fit in with the general order of things. For a start my knowledge of German, and by this time of some Austrian dialects too, was considered an asset which could play a useful part in news gathering and in helping run the little community's affairs.

The twelve consisted of one Australian, one New Zealander, three Scots, a Welshman and six Englishmen, including myself. The Camp Leader was John Thompson, a big burly, dark haired Scot, with a Charlie Chaplin moustache. He was the son of a builders' merchant in Scotland and a partner in his father's business. Vigorous and resolute, he was the outstanding personality of the camp and had been a Staff-Sergeant in the Royal Engineers at the time of his capture in Greece. He was also a skilled carpenter and amongst other things produced a splendid pine wood table for the camp. It was a good solid, well finished piece of furniture and when we all sat down to dine in the evening it added an unexpected touch of dignity to the meal.

The permanent "housekeeper" was a Regular Army Sergeant named Watts, known usually as "Dodo", probably because at 44 he was the oldest man there. I soon found that within the limits set by the ingredients available he was able to produce, among other things, a very acceptable chocolate cake for tea on Sundays.

The Australian, Jack Martin, was a lean, sunburnt, blue-eyed sheep farmer with a mop of unruly black hair. He became my regular partner at bridge after the evening meal but he was a persistent over-bidder. Jack missed feminine company more than anyone in the community and I think the fate of the sawmiller's wife often hung in the balance when she went outside to spend a late night final penny. This scrawny old harridan and her husband Kaspar lived in the house adjoining and like most houses in such remote areas it had no plumbing of any kind. The only other woman around was Mitzi who lived next door on the other side. But with two young children and a husband missing on the Eastern Front, she was thought to be above such desecration.

Kaspar, the master of the sawmill, was notionally in charge of the prisoners as far as work was concerned either in the sawmill or in the forests. He was a most unattractive person. Short, with one eye, a straw coloured wispy moustache, usually wearing a black hat with brim pulled down all round, he looked like a poor specimen of a walrus. He spoke always in a faint, flat murmuring voice and was a wholehearted, if gullible, Nazi supporter.

On the mountain side when the logs were sent down the races after the first snows, attempts were sometimes made to hit Kaspar with one. This was contrived by omitting to give the customary warning of "timber" or "achtung", but Kaspar, in spite of his one eye, was far too crafty to be caught napping.

To return to our household, the other notable character there was another Scot, John Anderson, who provided much of the humour in the camp and was also a very proficient amateur boxer. He had been runner-up in the light heavyweight class in the Stalag XVIIIA boxing championships. Sometimes he would ask me to spar with him for three rounds, using the Red Cross-provided gloves. My reach was slightly longer than his, but not being a boxer anywhere near his class, I often collected weighty blows. He hit me in the ribs or on the chest and consequently, they were not contests that I sought.

There was no doubt that within the limits imposed, it was a happy enough community of prisoners. In leisure time there were books and games to be enjoyed although there was not a single piece of flat ground anywhere in the vicinity where any kind of cricket or football could be played.

After watching them at work in the forest, it became clear that here was a little band of capable lumberjacks. Many of them in normal life were accustomed to working assiduously and turning out a proper job and it had become a built-in work attitude. Here in Austria it was again being demonstrated without them perhaps being aware for which cause and for which ultimate master their efforts were being made?

I made my debut on the lumber-jacking side after the first snows of autumn had fallen. The trees, mostly pines, were cut in a "schlag" or swathe about fifty to a hundred yards wide running from the top of the steep hillside down to the path below. After the trees had been felled, the branches were removed, then the bark which went for use in the tanneries. The trunks were then sawn into suitable lengths and assembled in piles, while long, thin ones remained uncut as "masts". When the snow came the logs were manoeuvred with spiked picks on to "races" made from saplings laid side by side to form a track. With snow and ice on these runways the logs would slither down the mountainside at great speed, often turning somersaults in mid-air, to finish up on a track below. Later the local contractors with horses and sledges would haul them away to the sawmill or elsewhere. It was a tough but healthy life set in magnificent scenery.

I felt that if I wanted to spend the remaining month or two of the war in these surroundings I would have to try to match the ability of my comrades. Otherwise I might be sent away to unpleasant work such as clearing rubble in bombed cities. There was also the safety aspect to be considered since stupidity or gross incompetence in manoeuvring some of the heavier logs on the slope might well have been the cause of serious injury to oneself or a fellow worker. My first efforts were woeful indeed. With my spiked pick I lunged again and again, missing the ice-coated logs that wormed and slithered around me. I felt rather like an English opening batsman facing the first venomous overs from the opening Australian bowlers. Sometimes I missed my footing altogether and landed upside down in the snow. Curiously enough this did not automatically evoke the peals of merriment and ribald comments which I expected from fellow prisoners. There were occasional laughs certainly but usually there was what seemed to be an indulgent attitude of professionals towards a novice.

At midday we all sat round a blazing log fire devouring the lunch we had brought with us, a billycan on the fire providing boiling water for the tea or coffee. Sometimes as we sat there, faces aglow before the blaze of the fire and the air tangy with the smell of burning pine logs, a million Yankee horsepower went roaring by overhead.

The months passed and still the Germans fought on and with the arrival of December there was still no sign of their immediate collapse. At Christmas time, if the weather is clear, the Austrian alpine scenery is quite enchanting. On the night of Christmas 1944 the view looking from the doorway of the prisoners' house was one of fantastic charm and splendour. Nestling on the steep side of a narrow valley the house looked upon wooded hills all round, many of the trees bearing a mantle of frosted snow. While the moon and stars made the frozen crust of the snow glitter wherever light reached, there was no stir of wind in the very cold air and all of nature seemed to sleep. Everywhere was covered with a thick blanket of white and over all, the silence, broken only by the rush of the bustling mountain stream cutting a dark ribbon through the snow.

Gazing at this picture of peace and serenity it was hard to realise that to the east, the west and the south millions of men of many nationalities, professional soldiers and amateurs, peasants and noblemen, clerks and artisans, men from city, mountain and plain, drawn from all corners of the world, were facing each other in bitter and savage conflict. They were fighting the final phases of a battle in which the destiny of all of them was being moulded. Many still living at that moment would not live to see the end. And for many more, the end, when it came, would bring despair and destitution.

The twelve of us had often talked at random about our own futures and all had generally agreed that they would be returning to their normal pre-war occupations although one or two had a very strong hankering for going to live in South Africa. We men from Britain had all visited there on the way to the Middle East theatre of war. The scenery and climate of South Africa and the generosity and friendliness of the South Africans had made a great impact upon all of us.

But one day someone threw up the novel idea that all of us should band together in a joint venture. This no doubt derived from the fact that, despite our varied backgrounds and living on top of one another, we had lived together as a harmonious community. The scheme put forward, which gave rise to many animated hours of discussion, was that we should pool our resources and build and operate a roadhouse with a swimming pool. It was unanimously agreed that John Thompson, the builder, would take absolute charge of the construction programme and instruct everyone else in the tasks which involved a great deal of hard labour.

It was agreed that when the premises had been established, each of us should perform the task to which he was most suited, without any feeling of inferiority regarding those doing jobs higher up the social scale. The Australian and the New Zealander, for instance, would take charge of a kitchen garden and any livestock that could be kept. I was to do the book-keeping and secretarial work but all would pitch in on the menial tasks, such as washing up or polishing floors, when the demands of their speciality jobs were not too pressing. Profits, if any, were to be divided in accordance with the amount of capital subscribed by each member.

Such were the Utopian ideas discussed in those distant days. The enthusiasm for the scheme was genuine and the Australians and New Zealanders had no apparent compunction about leaving their home countries in order to join us. Addresses were exchanged and it was agreed that we should all meet in London after the war with a view to getting the scheme launched. We did not know then, that all such plans would be frustrated by post-war restrictions on building.

The early new year brought an unexpected problem to the small band at our camp, and no doubt to nearly all other prisoners too. The Red Cross parcels, the mainstay of life, suddenly stopped. The explanation given was that the intense bombing had not only destroyed some of the supplies but was preventing the distribution of parcels by rail. Faced with this serious situation, the twelve of us went into consultation and decided that some of our surplus clothing and boots might be traded for food on the black market. The commandant was asked for permission for two or three of the prisoners to go for a walk in the surrounding countryside on Saturday afternoons and this was given. No escort was provided because it was mutually understood, though not in writing, that no attempt to escape would be made. So the opportunity was taken for myself and two others to call on a few nearby farms, all of which were very remote, away from any road and scarcely overlooked at all, to see what we would pick up. At nearly all the farms visited in this manner, a fairly friendly welcome was given to us.

Plain mountain folk, the farmers lived in very simple houses, most of which were without curtains or carpets, or any other luxury. A wooden table and forms, or benches against the wall, was about all the furniture usually seen in the living room. There was almost always a large stove which gave out a steady warmth, and of course double glazing was general. The only other items visible were perhaps a spinning wheel, and sometimes even a radio, with possibly the odd picture. And in most of the houses there was a religious icon in the corner.

A fairly typical bargain struck on these excursions was a live sheep for a pair of boots. The Austrians do not care for mutton or lamb and sheep seemed to be kept only for their wool, which was sometimes spun and woven on the farm.

Putting a pair of boots into the German agricultural economy and taking out a sheep did not seem a bad bargain, except indeed for the sheep. Keeping one of these creatures moving on the long trek home in the dusk was a trying business. With a rope round its neck and even with one man pulling and two pushing, or vice versa, progress was slow. Back at the camp the miserable sheep would be taken to the kitchen where the Australian and New Zealander in the household would slaughter it, skin it and have the meat sorted into joints in under half an hour. The first meal thus provided would be the liver, kidneys, sweetbreads, etc., and the bigger joints would be hoisted to the top of the nearest tall pine tree where they were not only out of sight but, in the cold winter days, as well preserved as in a refrigerator. There they would stay until required.

A cutlet or two to the commandant and something for the guard for their evening meals assured peaceful co-existence from those quarters, whilst we sat down to a really hearty dinner. The absence of the after-dinner smoke was, however, the great disappointment. All kinds of substitutes, from dried leaves, herbs, even to German ersatz coffee, were tried but gave little satisfaction.

On two occasions live calves were purchased by such barter and on this basis we managed to make the standard of living tolerable. Oscar Hey, the unflappable commandant so well remembered from the turmoils at the paper factory, took over the camp in early March.

From then on, together with the partial resumption of the supply of Red Cross parcels, the life of just waiting for the end was resumed. There were hordes of Allied bombers and fighters passing over each day and these occasionally ditched the odd bomb or expended a reserve petrol tank nearby, just to remind us that the struggle was still on.

From time to time I was required to do a little elementary clerical work at the Forsthaus, a fine residence at the top of a small mountain, where the Forstmeister in charge of the large estate lived.

Otto Praeger, who held this office, was a fairly insignificant little busybody, though a badge-carrying member of the Nazi Party, and therefore quite somebody in his own estimation. A Forstmeister is, however, a permanent civil servant of some real importance in the community and Praeger lived in far better style than anybody else for many miles around.

One day a Hungarian Staff Colonel from the Ministry of Defence in Budapest descended on Praeger with a fairly numerous staff. They had arrived in about half a dozen covered wagons each drawn by a pair of fine horses. Praeger complained volubly and at length to me about his obligation to look after his uninvited guest ("He is after all an ally," said Praeger) and bemoaned the necessity of providing food and facilities for his staff and fodder for the horses. Nearly every time he saw me in Praeger's house, when Praeger himself was not present, the Hungarian Colonel would ask me how far the Russians had advanced. He spoke equally fluently in either German or English and he clearly presumed that I was a regular listener to Allied news bulletins. This was indeed true, as whenever we could, we listened to the little radio belonging to the woman next door to the prisoners' house.

Although there was a far more adequate radio in the Forsthaus the Colonel no doubt felt that as the guest of a Nazi, tuning in to Allied news bulletins was not quite the thing to do! And the German news bulletins had seriously deteriorated by now. Then one morning when I arrived there was no sign of the Hungarians. The Russians at that date were reckoned to be about thirty or forty miles away and the Colonel and his wagon train had decided to beat it westwards, in order to avoid capture. Praeger too was beginning to get rather worried about his position and wondered what he could expect from the Allies. One of the prisoners promised to send him some cakes in prison!

In the course of further visits to the farms, to supplement the rations, a few deserters from the German Army were now encountered. These were mainly fellows who preferred to hide up in the remote parts of Austria, rather than be killed or captured in the last few weeks of the war on the Eastern Front. The farmers, possibly in some cases friends of those they were sheltering, showed no great anxiety in helping the deserters and allowed them to stay around. Since it was clear to all that the end was near, there were now no inhibitions at all in front of prisoners.

A deserter whom I met several times at one farm was an Austrian professor of pedagogy, from Graz. Until Hitler banned it, he had been a keen member of the Boy Scout movement, and an ardent admirer of its founder, Lord Baden Powell. The Professor was most anxious to discuss the coming post-war problems with us, particularly with regard to Russian policy under Stalin, whom he acknowledged as a great man. But he, rightly as it proved, had plenty of misgivings about the future.

At this farm we met twenty-two year old Greta, an Austrian girl from Graz, who with her elegant, stylish clothes looked rather out of place in those rustic surroundings. The daughter of a Social Democrat who was interned in a concentration camp, she had come up into the wilds to escape from the air raids on Graz, and to get a bit further away from the Russians. She moved and spoke with grace and charm and conversed easily and brightly in German or English. She was stimulating and unexpected company for our rather odd little gathering of three prisoners, visiting the farm "on business". The hearty farmer's wife, continually poured out some of her best cider for drinks all round.

With the first days of May 1945 there came tense excitement in the camp, as we waited almost hourly for the end of the war to come. The tension was the greater because it was so difficult to hear an Allied radio station on the little "People's receiver" belonging to our neighbour. Rumours were rife. Firm news was however received that the German Army under Field Marshal von Veitinghoff on the

Southern Front had surrendered and that Kaufmann, the Nazi Gauleiter of Carinthia, the neighbouring Austrian province, had stepped down.

But whilst it was true that Carinthia had indeed virtually dropped out of the war, the province of Styria where our little camp was situated was still in it. The Gauleiter, Dr. Siegfried Ueberreiter, had declared that all Styrians, men and women, would fight to the end until there were "no longer two stones standing one upon the other".

The Russians were now only thirty miles away to the east, the Americans were closing in from north and west, the Yugoslavs from the south-east and the British, furthest away but advancing very fast from the south. It looked as if Styria might be a hot seat if resistance was carried on to the last. The Germans were still putting up stiff resistance against the Russians, clinging to the forlorn hope that the Western Allies would join them in "the fight against Bolshevism".

The only actual evidence of Russian activity in our neighbourhood however was an occasional visit by a single Russian plane which dropped masses of leaflets in deserted forests! These leaflets called upon the Austrians to take a hand in their own liberation and were signed by Marshals Tobulkhin and Malinowsky.

With peace just around the corner each prisoner began to formulate views on how everything was going to work out in practice. Would we fly home or go by sea from Naples? Most thought that with massive Allied air fleets in Europe we would certainly fly.

"I'd like that little bastard, Kaspar, to try to get us to go to work when the ref' blows the whistle for full time," said Jack Martin, the Australian. "I've done all the hard yacker I'm ever going to do for the Huns. He can stuff his logs one by one."

Many of us had a queer, perhaps slightly nervous feeling about our forthcoming freedom. The impact, we thought, might be rather sudden and what would it feel like, after over four years, to go around and do things without an armed guard at hand? Would we be looking over our shoulders for him, as a habit? Would there in fact be an urge to rush around and in a mad flutter try to do all those things which had been beyond our reach for so long? Obviously it would require restraint and common sense on the part of every one not to plunge headlong into grabbing all the fruits of liberty in a mad fling.

But Japan cast a great shadow over our horizon in those last few days of the war in Europe, far greater than ever before. It was generally understood that priority had been given by the Allied leaders to settling accounts with Hitler and Mussolini first. From the news that was available it was obvious to many of us that Japan had made vast inroads into Far Eastern countries and if she continued to fight with fanaticism in defence of all this territory, the war could last for a long time yet.

Great hopes for speeding up the end were pinned on the Russians, who, it was thought, could play a very large part in building up overwhelming strength for the onslaught of Japan. In those days we had a warm regard for our Russian allies. Any slight misgivings about future Anglo-Soviet relations, derived more from the Russian aggression against Finland than from the bloody record of Bolshevism. We thought that all would be well in the future.

Regarding Germany, the overwhelming opinion among the British and Anzacs was that Hitler, the Nazis and all that they stood for, had to be ruthlessly wiped out. Very many believed too that Germany as a country and a nation would somehow cease to exist after the war and it would be absorbed and shared out between the victors.

I felt that this country in the heart of Europe, which had given so much to civilisation in the arts and sciences would, and must, continue to exist. I had seen a little of Germany before the war but it had left me with the impression of being a land of splendid cities and an industrious people. They had been for the most part more friendly and hospitable than some of the neighbouring European states. Above all, I felt that in music Germany had made the greatest contribution to the treasure chest of mankind and I hoped she would play a peaceful and constructive role in the post-war world.

The German Army, that mighty instrument of power, which had been the mainspring of all Hitler's territorial successes, was a special problem which would require the most careful attention. The Germans had fought with great skill and courage. Utter defeat brings its own feeling of desolation for troops but for those Germans who realised that they had fought for an evil cause the frustration was doubly intense.

It is all too easy for critics, in the security of the fireside armchair, to say that the Germans should not have allowed Hitler to get so far, and that they should have taken vigorous action against him. The German military, who gave this problem much thought, must have been plagued by a divided conscience. Many were appalled by the horrors of the concentration camps, the excesses in German-occupied territory, but equally they knew what fate would befall them if they raised a finger or voice against this barbarism. Under National Socialist law the practice of Sippenhaft was used by the Gestapo as a powerful deterrent. Under this code, anyone caught acting against the Nazis would not only feel the tortures of the Gestapo on his own flesh but he would know that his family, although perhaps quite innocent, would also suffer on the basis of shared responsibility. This, as the Nazis knew only too welt, acted not only as a deterrent, but led, often enough, to the denunciation of one relative by another.

German soldiers too were not only bound by their oath of allegiance to the State. They, like any others, were motivated by patriotism, to fight for what they thought to be the good of their country. These feelings were given greater fire in the early days when Hitler scored spectacular successes, some in face of weakness, dithering and even toleration on the part of the Western democracies.

I have often tried to imagine myself in the position of a German confronted with the fearful dilemma of either going along with the Nazis and rejoicing in their successes or taking an active part against the regime. I have always been thankful that such an awful choice never arose for me and that I was born and bred in a country where terror belongs to the past.

There were, of course, several attempts at overthrowing Hitler or taking his life. They failed either through lack of resolution or because of the extraordinarily kind fate which seemed to watch over the Fuehrer. The brave Germans who carried out the July plot, and who had attempted earlier ones, suffered a grisly end that is too horrible to contemplate.

In the end Hitler shot himself on 30th April and on 7th May the surrender was signed. I heard of Hitler's death on Kaspar's radio and none of our Austrian neighbours made any comment. They appeared to be either too unworldly or too stupid to realise the consequences.

On the morning of 8th May, with no thought of doing any kind of work, I sat by the radio listening to the local broadcasting station, which produced nothing but music. About mid-morning, what seemed an interminable programme of Unterhaltungsmusik (light music) was interrupted and it was announced that a Professor Berger would give a talk. I groaned inwardly halfexpecting a lecture on butterflies or something equally irrelevant. But in a calm, rather flat voice the Professor announced that the war was over, and that from that moment all Nazi organisations were illegal. He added that it was desired that the occupation of the country by the Allies should take place peacefully and that civilians should keep off the roads and furthermore, there should be no interference with retreating German units.

I left the house to give the news to my friends. We had known that the end was close at hand for some days from news bulletins especially after the death of Hitler, yet it came as a shock! Oddly enough I was reminded suddenly of a little song which I had learnt from the Austrians about two years previously which was a parody on a folksong with an attractive, wistful melody. It ran like this:

> *Es geht alles vorueber*
> *Es geht alles vorbei,*
> *In April geht Hitler*
> *In Mai die Partei.*

Which very roughly translated into English might read as:

> *Everything comes to an end,*
> *Everything passes away,*
> *In April goes Hitler*
> *And the Party in May.*

And so it had come to pass... nobody on that sensational day, even before the formal announcement which I reported, had had any intentions of doing any work. Now with the news that the war really was over emotion gained sway. Hats were thrown into the air, backs were ferociously slapped and excited discussions began as to what form the physical liberation would take. What would be the route home and when would we get there? And – to us perhaps the most important point of all – which of the liberating armies would get to us first?

For some technical reason, the cease-fire was not to take effect until twenty-four hours later on the Eastern Front. Nevertheless, according to my reckoning, the Russians were the nearest to us by far. So, from my minute Russian vocabulary I hastily concocted a phrase meant to convey to liberating Russians that we were British Commonwealth troops. There was a risk of being taken as the enemy, as a year or two previously whilst travelling in a train a dear old Austrian lady, no doubt confused by the great variety of uniforms around her in the police state, had thought that my British battledress was the brown uniform of the Storm Troopers! It was far more amusing than flattering but I certainly did not want any erring Georgian or Mongol to make the same mistake.

There was, however, very little that we could celebrate with in any practical form. We had no drink and no musical instruments, and a completely sober and silent celebration is not quite the thing! We were in a very remote corner of the province with just four or five rather broken-down Austrians of the woodcutting fraternity as neighbours. And some among us were still mindful of the fact that Japan was not beaten by a long way.

After it had been arranged for the twelve prisoners to pack up and return to Stalag XVIIIA on the following morning, I went off to see Greta. I had spent the last night with her in a hay loft and I said good-bye to her with very mixed feelings!

XII *The Victors March In*

Our guard was given instructions by the Commandant to take us back to the Stalag and to be responsible for our safety on the journey. The only transport available was a lorry laden with boards from the saw-mill which were to be delivered to Wolfsberg, the neighbouring town. The lorry, propelled by wood gas, set off with the guard and the twelve of us all in very high spirits and singing lustily while perched on top of the high load of timber.

The guard was a simple rural Austrian whose one interest it seemed, after delivering us safely to the main camp, was to get back to his small-holding in Styria, especially to see whether his pigs were still safe and sound!

Conversation among the ex POWs was light and fanciful and was inspired by the novelty of freedom or something very near to it.

"Fancy being able to walk into a shop to buy a packet of Players," said John Thompson, incredulously. He was a heavy smoker and had tried all kinds of substitutes for tobacco from dried alpine weeds to tree bark and German substitute coffee.

"And chocolate eclairs, look you," said the rather tubby Welshman, who was especially fond of his food.

"What price the Master Race now?" asked Jack, the Australian, who gazed around at the hordes of retreating and dispirited Germans. "What a day for us! It seems almost unbelievable that it's come at last, fair dinkum."

"I wouldn't mind coming back here to lord it over them for a while," John said. "I'd have dozens of slaves jumping around, just to took after my personal wishes."

On joining the main road, the Packstrasse, we were soon amongst the dense columns of the German Army retreating westwards, to avoid capture by the Russians. The German troops were battle-weary and bitter. How bitter we did not realise until we had very nearly made a fatal mistake. The Germans were for the most part still heavily armed and in no mood for humour or trifling. As the timber lorry passed one horse-drawn vehicle packed with German soldiers, the New Zealander in our little band called out some derisive remarks. The German soldier sitting next to the man with the reins took violent exception to this and, swiftly putting one up the spout of his rifle, took aim at us at about twenty yards range. Thirteen heads went down in a flash, but from the corner of my eye I saw the rifle tugged away by a companion at the very last moment. That was a very lucky escape and it was unanimously decided that there would be no more silly provocations. Discretion is said to be the better part of valour and this is especially true if you have no gun and the other fellow has.

About a mile further on, to everyone's surprise and our unrestrained delight, the advancing British Army was sighted. It was represented by three armoured cars and a despatch rider! The British were the furthest away by our calculations and we were almost resigned to liberation by the Russians – they being the nearest approaching Allies. This encounter was quite unexpected and the tiny column, flying white balloons as a sign of no combat, was advancing very slowly against the mass of Germans going the other way.

The road was quite inadequate to carry such heavy traffic and the little spearhead was completely stuck in a traffic jam. It was given a mighty cheer by the twelve of us as they looked oddly isolated amidst the swarm of Germans. We leapt down from the lorry and slapped the back of the despatch rider, causing the dust to rise in clouds from his battledress. The head of an officer nonchalantly emerged from the turret of one of the armoured cars and a very cultured voice casually enquired: "Are you chaps all right down there?" Were we all right? We most certainly were!

"Good on you, sport," Jack bawled out in the familiar way that Australians always seemed to address officers, "Give my regards to the Ruskies if you meet them."

The little force then began to edge its way forward again, its object apparently being to establish contact with the Russians in Graz. Its progress was marked dramatically by Austrian national flags, which jerked out from the top window or balcony of nearly every house as the conquerors came level. The Austrians never had liked the Germans and no longer needed to pretend that they did.

We found that Stalag XVIIIA had also been "conquered", by a very small British force – a major and two sergeants who had dropped by parachute. When the commandant offered to surrender the camp he was told by the major to maintain his guards and administration until the prisoners were in a position to take over the camp. This was to be done without any unseemly incident. Both the prisoners and their guards accepted the need for a smooth transition. Nobody cut loose, and nobody got hurt. So when our small party at last reached Stalag XVIIIA, we found it a very different place from that which I had left in the autumn.

The problems of feeding the thousands of mouths of many nationalities gathered in the Stalag was a great one. We were told that it was to be solved by the American Air Force, which was expected to drop supplies by parachute. The supplies were supposed to come down in a dropping zone marked out nearby. However, large numbers of heavy canisters were dropped on the camp itself. Having lived through years of bombing on a massive scale, this form of supply dropping made us all jittery. Anything which dropped from the skies, including the canisters was treated as a threat. As they descended all eyes were on them, and if it looked as though there was danger of being hit in one area of the camp there was a surge of scared souls into another corner. The canisters were, in fact, formidable missiles. It took four men to lift them, and one did actually go through the roof of one of the barracks, but luckily nobody was hurt.

Worse was to follow. A "free drop" of smaller packages sent people scurrying for safety at an even more frantic speed. The atmosphere was further gingered up by low flying American Mustang fighters which swooped over the camp rooftops, presumably with the object of raising our spirits! It was kind of them, no doubt, but we would have been far happier without them.

Near the end of 1944 the camp had been badly hit by bombs, causing numerous deaths. Other camps had suffered casualties too, and it was only natural that those who had been bombed in captivity, usually without the protection of any air-raid shelter, should suffer from nerves in any form of aerial bombardment.

A day later there was a little ceremonial parade of tremendous import: the camp guards laid down their arms and marched off and the weapons were taken up by former British Commonwealth and French prisoners, who then shared guard duty at all points of the camp. I found myself on duty with an amiable Frenchman, in one of the watch towers armed with an old type Czech Bren gun with which, as it happened, neither of us was familiar. Fortunately nothing disturbed our watch.

By now the British Army was beginning to arrive in a greater strength and a company of the London-Irish Regiment stayed in the camp for one evening. They staged a little drill parade in their plumes and kilts to the music of their pipes. The Russians were quite fascinated by this and thought the "dancing" (slow marching) was very entertaining. The Russians in fact welcomed every conquering Briton they saw with prolonged hand clapping.

The following day a note of emergency was struck when a little force of ex prisoners-of-war was marched down to the former German HQ in nearby Wolfsberg. Their instructions were to man the defences, because an attack by Tito's forces was thought to be imminent. Tito at that time was trying to stake a claim to portions of Austrian territory and there was, as a result, a bit of skirmishing between the British and the Yugoslavs.

Austrian officers, still of course in their German Army uniform, were asked to take a part in the defence of Wolfsberg, and I was kept busy interpreting British Army orders to them. If the need should arise, reinforcement would be made by paratroop units, as they could fly in from the south within a few hours.

Whilst these preparations were going on the process of disarming the Waffen SS was being enforced, another task entrusted to former prisoners. SS units in the vicinity had been instructed to report to Wolfsberg and to lay down their arms there. The weapons of course came in useful in preparation for any Yugoslav attack. Many of the guns put down in the huge piles were far more modern and complicated than anything we former prisoners had seen before. Each of us grabbed the best he could find for himself, our first idea being to establish authority over the SS who were being disarmed.

As it happened this was not difficult, for several reasons. They had had enough, and anyway orders were orders, even if it meant surrendering. Most of the picked men of the Waffen SS had been lost in battle and many of those we saw were simple young peasants who had been dragooned into the force. Our second idea was that we might as well have the best weapons available for any other eventualities which might arise.

Most of us, however, had little idea how to handle these strange and complex weapons, and I for one was glad not to meet any S.S. man who was unwilling to be disarmed, particularly after dark! But all went smoothly as the SS laid down their arms in a mood of sullen apathy. The attack from Tito never came, and a day or so later British Army lorries arrived and took the liberated British prisoners to Klagenfurt airfield, to be flown from there to Naples.

American transport aircraft carried us on this flight and the American crews were very sympathetic when they discovered how long we had been behind barbed wire, and, as ever, they were generous in a variety of ways. During the flight the pilot invited two at a time to come into his compartment for a better view of the landscape. The weather was fair and the route an interesting one over Trieste and Rome. I had the good fortune to be with the pilot when he asked: "Does anybody want to see Rome?" So down we went to what must have been a forbidden height over the city and made a couple of circuits during which the main features were pointed out to us. Just over four years previously I had wandered round Athens at leisure and now I was "doing" Rome in a minute or two!

On leaving the aircraft and while walking to the reception office a member of one of the British Women's services asked me: "Would you like some cigarettes and chocolate?" I realised suddenly that it had been nearly five years since I had heard an English girl's voice. It was quite a day!

EPILOGUE

In Naples we were debriefed on our experiences in captivity and I was told by my Commanding Officer to make a full report on my intelligence activities. The journey from Naples in Italy to Brize Norton in Oxfordshire was made in the bomb bay of a Lancaster bomber piloted by an RAF officer who must have been at least 20 years of age. He pleaded with us not to touch any of "these wires" in the cramped space assigned to the ex-prisoners. In Brize Norton we were given leave passes and double ration cards which pleased my parents when I arrived home. At the same time we had a pay parade, presided over by a colonel who apart from giving us Army back-pay, honoured our German "monopoly" or "bingo" vouchers which had been issued in return for our labour. There had been nothing we wished to buy and those prisoners who had worked steadily over the years were cashing in with unspent vouchers. Ironically, those who had made persistent attempts to escape and had spent time on the run followed by time in prison cells, received little by comparison. I was one who protested angrily at this policy but was howled down by those who were benefiting from the system.

On the way home I took the opportunity of visiting an elderly aunt and uncle in Buckinghamshire who had written to me often over the years. The aunt had been a Suffragette and a Fabian in her earlier life. The uncle was a palaeontologist, geologist and had written a book jointly on anthropology with H.G. Wells when the latter was a serious scientist. My aunt was not very fond of Wells because on any visit to her house he would seek to squeeze the housemaid's bottom.

It was when I got home to my parents that I received an acknowledgement of my services to MI 9/19, typed on war time flimsy paper and using the wrong dates. I have a cousin who spent many years compiling our family history and for the record I sought to have the error in dates corrected. I approached our local MP who at that time was Maurice Macmillan, son of the former Prime Minister. He was very pleased to take up my case with the then Minister of Defence in the Labour Government at that time. The Minister was really not interested in this matter and I was fobbed off, to the dismay of Macmillan.

At the end of my six weeks leave I was ordered to report to an army camp in Sussex. This was for retraining in the weapons and equipment of the day, which for the most part, bore little resemblance to those with which we had been sent to war in the first place. Much of our original small arms, artillery and signals systems had derived from the First World War. Now, we were told, we were to be sent to the Far East to take part in the war against Japan. Not many weeks later that war came to an end with the dropping of two atom bombs upon Japan and VJ Day was declared for celebration. Our army camp was situated near Haywards Heath in Sussex, about an hour's train journey from London but all ranks were confined to barracks for VJ day. I was very conscious that this was a special day in world history and was determined to join the fun in London. If one can break out of a prison camp, the ordinary British Army camp should present little difficulty. Consequently I joined the enormous crowds milling around Trafalgar Square and Buckingham Palace and even joined in the dancing with bus conductresses from Lancashire. The return journey to camp was on a train leaving London at about 5 a.m. the next morning and the first parade that day was physical training!

With the end of the war against Japan I was not demobilised because I belonged to an age group which numbered about 1,000,000 men and the British economy was in no state to absorb that number. Thus there followed a resettlement course which involved visiting various industries with a view to later employment. Numerous approaches were made offering me a commission in the Army but I felt this only put off the day when one had to seek employment in the civilian sector.

In 1946 1 wrote to Zeller to enquire about his welfare and he replied with a very genial letter. A translation of his letter is in the Appendix together with copies of the original German text. When finally demobilised in mid 1946 I was offered a post in British Intelligence which I could not refuse and was posted to Hamburg – or what was left of it. As everyone knows, Stalin took over where Hitler left off and the striking resemblance between their two regimes are well documented in Professor Alan Bullock's "Hitler/Stalin Parallel lives".

So there was more work to be done. The Russians were only 80 miles from Hamburg, the main British supply base and there were times in the years to follow when the fate of Europe hung on a knife edge once more.

It was in the Hamburg General Hospital that I had the chance to meet German Field Marshal von Rundstedt.[6] I had just had my tonsils removed and became aware that von Rundstedt and his wife were living under British protective custody in a house in the grounds. He wore a British battle dress and was followed everywhere at a distance away of about 20 yards by a British soldier. The Russians wanted him to be handed over to them but the British refused. German is not the ideal language to speak with my still very sore throat but I thought that von Rundstedt could be very useful to know. With his very high reputation in ex Wehrmacht circles he could put me in touch with useful people. He told me that while he was a POW in Wales he had written a book in conjunction with Liddell Hart called *The Other Side of the Hill* but as Liddell Hart stuttered and von Rundstedt's English was not too good, progress had been slow.

---

[6] Field Marshal von Rundstedt, senior Field Marshal of the German Army, the commander who captured France in 1940, later commanded Army Group South in Russia and was later commander-in-chief in the West. ' A short description of von Rundstedt's career appears in the Appendix.

It was some years before my conscience urged me to visit Zeller and accordingly as a covering ploy about my intending visit, I wrote to the secretary at the paper factory. My visit was most welcome and I was given a good lunch by the works General Manager and entertained for an evening by two members of the works fire service – my visit was reported in the local press. However, I could not find Zeller and nobody seemed to offer any help. I even walked around the local cemetery in my search.

When I visited Stalag XVIIIA I found an empty space but I remembered that when we prisoners were there, there had been one specially attractive view. This was the turreted castle on the nearby mountain with its own mausoleum a few yards further along. It belonged to Graf Otto Henckel von Donnersmarck. While I was there, I decided to visit it. The Graf was not in residence but a housekeeper was quick to tell me that they were still trying to get the stains from the parquet flooring. Apparently, the British had used the castle as a local H.Q. and had stubbed out their cigarette ends on the floor. My thoughts probably dwelt for a moment on the cartloads of Russian corpses carried out of our Stalag and compared that with the seriousness of the current complaints. Down in the pretty town of Wolfsberg I had a coffee in a cafe and finding that the owner belonged to my generation I began a fairly bland conversation. It transpired he had been a Nazi of some standing and he was indignant that the British had banged him up in the same camp which we all knew so well. He also asserted with some heat that Churchill was the biggest war criminal of the lot!

I left the service of MI 6 in 1958 and joined Shell/BP in their headquarters in the Strand, London. I left the Shell Company in 1977 and worked for the Institute of Electrical Engineers, translating technical journals from German and Russian into English. Some years later I became aware of the Association for a Free Russia which I promptly joined. It was headed by a Russian family and meetings were mostly held in the crypt of the Russian Orthodox Church in Exile in London. The membership consisted of a great variety of Australian and Canadian Russians but the British were in the majority. It was an association dedicated to reaching hearts and minds and the intelligentsia in the USSR were bombarded with our leaflets. Because I can write in the Russian script I would often spend Saturday afternoons and evenings addressing envelopes of all shapes, colours and sizes. It was thought that those addressed in Russian stood a better chance of getting past the KGB.

The Association had many patrons ranging from Russians to British MPs from all parties. Very prominent among such MPs were Baroness Cox and Lady Olga Maitland who both made visits to Russia to encourage those striving towards a genuine democracy. These two valiant ladies must have given the KGB an acute pain in the fundament but they could scarcely be arrested. On one occasion in the Gorbachev era, I was permitted to join the strike leaders of the Russian coal miners who were invited to attend a session with an MP in the House of Commons and answer questions about the USSR.

I had long believed that I would never see the end of the Bolshevist Empire and the Warsaw Pact in my lifetime. I watched, with amazement, the pictures on television as Yeltsin made his courageous stand to defy the tanks leading the putsch in 1991. He told the tank commander Yevdokimov that he, Yeltsin, was the elected president (Gorbachev had been self appointed) and that he would give the orders now.

One of the most effective efforts of the Association was to collect money which enabled our friends in the USSR to buy a second-hand printing press. Once it was suspected that a putsch was on they printed posters exhorting the citizens of Moscow to "come and defend your Parliament". The people responded and built barricades with any available materials – including off-duty buses. Yeltsin had sent a Russian Treasury official on a normal treasury mission to London but gave him a personal message for John Major, the Prime Minister, regarding the approach of the crisis. This was delivered with the help of the Association. The Prime Minister gave immediate backing to Yeltsin on the street outside No. 10 Downing Street, yet the French President backed the putsch.

Some days later three of our Russian friends who had been on those barricades as events unfolded in Moscow and St. Petersburg, spoke to a large gathering in London giving a ball by ball account of the great drama.

The British and the Americans did a lot of bellyaching to obtain the release of special prisoners from Gorbachev's gulags. As a result of these activities I met some notable Russians and amongst them, were:

Bernomansky, a lawyer who studied with Gorbachev, who having been given the task of defending Brezhnev's hair raising criminal son, thought the job a bit dicey and defected.

The Chief Psychiatrist of the USSR who was sentenced to seven years in a gulag when he protested that the KGB were misusing psychiatry by asserting, 'If you don't agree with the Communist Party you must be mad and such people were given "appropriate" injections in mental homes'.

Irina Ratuschinskaya, is regarded as the greatest Russian poet today. She was sentenced to seven years in the Gulag basically for her Christian beliefs. The climax was her poem "This is not my Russia". They tried to freeze her into submission and she only had to admit she had made a mistake and she would have been released. When I asked her how she managed to speak such reasonable English, she said she had learned much by borrowing Kipling's "Just So" stories from another prisoner. She knew a little English and using the book she had been able to achieve a modest vocabulary.

APPENDICES

TRANSMITTING INTELLIGENCE MESSAGES.

At the time that I was in the Stalag, I was never aware of the method used to communicate our information to Allied Intelligence. Some years ago I made two visits to the British Public Records office and found the curator of the M19/MI19 files extremely coy about what could be viewed. One file would not be available until 2045!

However, the following researchers uncovered the fact that most intelligence material gained by prisoners in various POW camps was probably sent back to Allied intelligence by coded letters home. It should be noted that in 1979, many records were not yet open and in their book "M19", Foot and Langley do not mention Stalag XVIIIA:

With the help of a Foreign Office expert called Hooker, Winterbottom and his colleagues developed a code called HK through which several people were communicating with London from Germany by November 1940.... Like several codes developed later HK was at once fairly simple to use, and in skilled hands unusually hard to detect. All the user had to do was to indicate by the fashion in which he wrote the date that the letter contained a message, show by his opening words which part of the code he was using, and then write an apparently chatty letter, from which an inner meaning could be unravelled with the code's help.

A POST-WAR LETTER FROM "ZELLER"

Frantschach

7 October 1946

Dear friend Greville!

"My very best thanks to you for your letter and I must tell you that I was very pleased to hear that you are still alive. I have so much to report, however, I must restrict myself to what is most necessary. Therefore we should start with the place where we parted company. The man in charge of Machine No. II, Lyssy, died of hunger in 1944 in the concentration camp in Dachau. The farmer with the golden tooth, named Russmann, was arrested by the Gestapo and was murdered in a Berlin punishment prison. The charge was that he had assisted an English POW to escape. Grillitsch and his daughter Anni were imprisoned for 3 months; a Nazi had reported to the Gestapo that Rushton (Tasmanian) and Oakes (British) had hidden in his hayloft. We were able however to fix up a perfect alibi for Grillitsch and the Gestapo had to release them.

When I tell you that Jedlichka and Medwed as well as Liebentritt and Steiner (badge carrying Nazi Party members) who had not only accused the English POW Nix of starting the (factory) fire, but had struck English prisoners and treated

206

workers from the East (Russians and Ukrainians) *like animals, are still free, doing the same job with the same rank, you can imagine the feelings of the workers. I must add that immediately after the British troops arrived I made a report to the FSS (British Field Security Service) in Wolfsberg. The Nazi Works Directors, Vogele and Franke were sacked.*

Dear friend Greville! You know the attitude of the workers in Frantschach. Now just imagine:- I was commandeered with 150 workers to build a defensive position on the Pack Road, that is the one that leads to Graz. We had the task of blowing up this lovely mountain road in order to prevent the Russians from entering Carinthia. You can imagine what a show that was. The work achieved in 8 weeks amounted to what could be accomplished in 1 day. Whatever was accomplished by 150 men in daylight under the direction of the SS was destroyed at night by 5 of us. As the motorised SS of Styria had to return to Carinthia we managed to smash in the fuel tanks of 3 or 4 vehicles and in 10 minutes all traffic on the whole of the Pack Road came to a halt. Not even a pedestrian, let alone a vehicle, could get through. You cannot imagine the chaos that reigned in the motorised SS. You can, however, imagine the joy for us when the first English tank arrived. I offered the two English soldiers a 2 litre jug of the best Lavant Valley matured cider. They gulped it down in one go. All around there were plenty of SS fascists. In Carinthia these Hitler bandits were hunted like hares in a free hunt. From the south came English troops, from the east the Russians and from the west the

American and French troops. We witnessed the collapse of the "1000 Year Reich" just as we imagined it would happen and just as we said it would happen. Now the war, if that is what we can call this crime against humanity, is over. Millions of young people are dead. Desolation and destruction were the only results of this madness. Let us hope that the whole of humanity will not believe in such madness again. We in Austria have suffered much in the events of 1939–45 and today we are a shuttlecock in world events but we have one thing that outweighs all else. That is we are Austrians again and no longer Ostmark. (The disintegration of Austria when it was annexed to Germany in 1936). We can speak freely again without running the risk of landing tomorrow in a concentration camp.

Dear friend Greville! Should you happen to meet your friends – Oakes, Rushton (Tasmanian), Nix and whatever the others are called, please give them kind regards from me and my friends. Should you however come to Austria then please don't forget to pay me a visit, I would really be delighted. Regarding your greetings to my family, I shall pass them on. We are all alive and well and thank you heartily for your regards.

Now we friends in Frantschach send most hearty greetings and hope to hear from you again.

Greetings

The mutual trust that grew between "Zeller" and myself had continued and had stood the test of time.

FIELD MARSHAL GERD VON RUNDSTEDT

My first mission of intelligence gathering, given me by Lawrence, was to find out the identity of the German C-in-C on the Southern front. That man was reported to be von Rundstedt. Ironically, I was to meet him later and this short appendix describes the man:

Field Marshal von Rundstedt was the most senior Field Marshal in the German Army and he, with notably two of his contemporaries, FM von Manstein and FM Guderian (the only one who could shout back at Hitler and get away with it) played leading roles in all the brilliant victories in the first years of the war. All three were ardent disciples of Captain Liddell Hart, the British military historian and military thinker who propounded ideas for the use of highly mobile armoured formations in the art of warfare. In fact von Rundstedt wrote a book in conjunction with Liddell Hart, entitled The other side of the hill.

All three Germans were at various times either sacked or they resigned but were then recalled when Hitler had made an awful mess in his conduct of the war. In army circles von Rundstedt was well known for referring to Hitler as "that Bohemian corporal in Berlin".

In the lightning victory over France, von Manstein was Chief of Staff to von Rundstedt and produced a brilliant plan for the attack. After the victory

Figure 14: Field Marshal vonRrundstedt, senior Field Marshal of the
German army.

Hitler claimed all the credit and declared himself to be the "greatest field marshal of all time".

After France, von Rundstedt went on to conquer the Ukraine in the war against the Soviet Union, taking over 660,000 prisoners in Kiev. At the time of the invasion of Normandy in 1944, von Rundstedt was Commander in Chief of the West and under him, Field Marshal Rommel commanded Army Group B in Normandy. The tactics Rommel and von Rundstedt employed for meeting the expected invasion, were diametrically opposed. Rommel believed that the invading armies must be defeated on the sea or on the beaches and German forces should be brought up behind the Atlantic Wall. Against this view von Rundstedt said he had a poor opinion of the Atlantic Wall and in any case the German Army was not a fortress army with a Maginot Line philosophy, it was an army of thrust and manoeuvre. Forces should be held well back until the main enemy thrust had been identified and then everything thrown at it with every man on wheels, even if they were bicycle wheels. Rommel and von Rundstedt's views were irreconcilable and Hitler had to be called in to arbitrate and fatally, he compromised. There was a great divergence of opinion amongst senior German commanders as to where the invasion would take place, most thinking it would be via the shortest route – the Pas de Calais, although Hitler tipped Normandy. British Intelligence played a vital role in this monumental operation. German Intelligence had infiltrated an agent into Britain who transferred his allegiance unreservedly to the British. He was a radio operator given the codename, by the British, of Garbo. His transmission contained a large measure of disinformation, enhanced by scraps of genuine value, which were easily verifiable by the Germans. One message gave the real date of the invasion but so finely timed that by the time it had been decoded on French soil and re-encoded for Berlin and then decoded there, – the invasion was actually happening. Hitler was so pleased with this star performance that Garbo was awarded the Iron Cross over the airways and M.I.6. collected his pay from Lisbon as usual. The next Garbo transmission urged the Germans not to pay too much attention to the "diversionary" landing in Normandy as the main effort would come in the Pas de Calais, where the 15th Tank Army under General von Salmuth was waiting for it.

Hitler always retained control of tank formations and they would only be released to field commanders with his permission. At 4 a.m. on the day of the Normandy landing von Rundstedt telephoned Hitler and requested the release of two tank formations. Hitler declined saying he did not think that Normandy was the main invasion effort, went to bed and slept until the afternoon. When the truth dawned some days later von Salmuth's tanks made the laborious journey, in daylight through battlefield rubble, to Normandy and were badly mauled on the way. Even so, as the Duke of Wellington said of Waterloo, the invasion had been "a damn close run thing".

In most of the working camps when I was a POW it was often possible to obtain a German newspaper and the first item I would read would be the military communiqué from the German High Command. They were not very imbued with propaganda and often disclosed more than could be obtained from BBC sources. More than once there was a reference in Normandy to "a curtain of fire from 15-inch naval guns through which no man or machine could pass". Rommel moved closer to von Rundstedt's thinking of keeping the main forces back out of range of the Navy's guns but of course there was still the endless bombardment from the air and artillery to contend with. A conference with Hitler was necessary before any kind of withdrawal could be ordered. Hitler insisted they should not retreat one yard. Later a second conference was called with the same agenda and the same result except that Hitler ranted about new bombs which could destroy battleships, new aircraft and weapons which would turn the tide and the like. A dejected Rommel and von Rundstedt returned to France to find that the SS 21st Tank Army had been defeated by the British and Canadians and was in a state of total exhaustion. At this point von Rundstedt telephoned FM Keitel, (Hitler's lackey) but nominally Chief of the High Command and told him that this situation "was the beginning of the end". "What is there to do?" asked Keitel. Von Rundstedt gave his famous answer "Make peace you bloody idiots".

Shortly after this von Rundstedt was given another decoration and told that he had "resigned". His replacement was Field Marshal Guenther von Kluge, the man who got so very close to Moscow in 1941. Hitler knew that von Kluge's loyalty to him was very suspect but the High Command persuaded him to give his consent to the appointment on the grounds of necessity. The overwhelming priority of von Kluge, personally, was to seek peace terms with the Western

Powers. His mind, however, was much troubled by the fact that in France SS tank divisions exceeded the number of German Army tank units and whereas the German Army might well obey orders from their Commander in Chief to cease fire the SS divisions' first loyalty might be to Hitler. Field Marshal von Kluge was absent from his post, making peace enquiries, when Hitler telephoned him. His absence of course was deeply suspicious and he was summoned to report to Berlin. On the way he stopped for a picnic lunch, walked into the woods and committed suicide.

Once again von Rundstedt was recalled at the age of 71 to lead the German attack through the Ardennes with the ultimate aim of recapturing the port of Antwerp. This was a nasty surprise for the British and the Americans but the attack was brought to a halt and von Rundstedt said "It was the last twitch of the chicken after its neck had been wrung".

Also published by Woodfield...

The following titles are all available in high-quality softback format

RAF HUMOUR

Bawdy Ballads & Dirty Ditties of the RAF • A huge collection of the bawdy songs and rude recitations with which RAF personnel would entertain one-another in off-duty hours in WW2. Sure to amuse any RAF veteran. (uncensored – strictly adults only!) *"Not for the frail, the fraightfully posh or proper gels – but great fun for everyone else!"* **£9.95**

Upside Down Nothing on the Clock • Dozens of jokes and anecdotes contributed by RAF personnel from AC2s to the top brass... one of our best sellers. *"Highly enjoyable."* **£6.00**

Upside Down Again! • Our second great collection of RAF jokes, funny stories and anecdotes – a great gift for those with a high-flying sense of humour! *"Very funny indeed."* **£6.00**

Was It Like This For You? • A feast of humorous reminiscences & cartoons depicting the more comical aspects of life in the RAF. *"Will bring back many happy memories. Highly recommended."* **£6.00**

I Have Control • former RAF Parachute instructor **Edward Cartner** humorously recalls the many mishaps, blunders and faux-pas of his military career. *Superb writing; very amusing indeed.* **£9.95**

Who is in Charge Here...? • Former RAF Parachute instructor **Edward Cartner** regales us with more inglorious moments from the latter part of his military career as a senior officer. *Superb writing; very amusing indeed.* **£9.95**

MILITARY MEMOIRS & HISTORIES – THE POST-WAR PERIOD

A History of the King's Flight & The Queen's Flight • An illustrated history of the RAF's Royal illustrious squadron, responsible for the air transport of the Royal family from its inception in 1936 to its disbandment in 1995. **£15.00**

Flying the Waves • **Richard Pike** describes his eventful second career as a commercial helicopter pilot, which involved coastguard Air/Sea Rescue operations in the Shetlands and North Sea. **£9.95**

From Port T to RAF Gan • The history of the RAF's most deserted outpost is comprehensively and entertainingly charted by **Peter Doling**, a former RAF officer who served on Gan in the 1970s. Many photos, some in colour. **£20.00**

Korea: We Lived They Died • Former soldier with Duke of Wellington's Regt **Alan Carter** reveals the appalling truth of front-line life for British troops in this now forgotten war. *Very funny in places too.* **£9.95**

Meteor Eject! • Former 257 Sqn pilot [1950s] **Nick Carter** recalls the early days of RAF jets and his many adventures flying Meteors, including one very lucky escape via a Martin-Baker ejector seat... **£9.95**

Pluck Under Fire • Eventful Korean War experiences of **John Pluck** with the Middlesex Regiment. **£9.95**

Return to Gan • Michael Butler's light-hearted account of life at RAF Gan in 1960 and the founding of 'Radio Gan'. *Will delight those who also served at this remote RAF outpost in the Indian Ocean.* **£12.00**

The Spice of Flight • Former RAF pilot **Richard Pike** delivers a fascinating account of flying Lightnings, Phantoms and later helicopters with 56, 43(F) & 19 Sqns in the RAF of the 1960s & 70s. **£9.95**

Tread Lightly into Danger • Bomb-disposal expert **Anthony Charlwood**'s experiences in some of the world's most dangerous hotspots (Kuwait, Iraq, Lebanon, Somalia, etc) over the last 30 years. **£9.95**

MILITARY MEMOIRS & HISTORIES – WORLD WAR 1 & 2

A Bird Over Berlin Former Lancaster pilot with 61 Sqn **Tony Bird DFC** tells a remarkable tale of survival against the odds during raids on the German capital & as a POW. *"An incredible-but-true sequence of events."* **£9.95**

Algiers to Anzio with 72 & 111 Squadrons Former engineer officer **Greggs Farish**'s diary and photos are a superb historical record of RAF squadron life during Operation 'Husky' – the invasion of Sicily/Italy in 1943. **£9.95**

An Erk's-Eye View of World War 2 • former 'instrument basher' **Ted Mawdsley** salutes the work of the RAF ground crews of WW2, who played a vital role in keeping the RAF's aircraft flying in often adverse conditions. **£9.95**

An Illustrated History of RAF Waddington Former crewmember of the famous Battle of Britain flight Ray Leach has researched the wartime history of this important RAF base. Many photos. *"A superb achievement."* **£20.00**

A Lighter Shade of Blue • A former Radar Operator **Reg O'Neil** recalls his WW2 service in Malta and Italy with 16004 AMES – a front-line mobile radar unit. *'Interesting, informative and amusing.'* **£9.95**

A Shilling's Worth of Promises • Delightfully funny memoirs of **Fred Hitchcock,** recalling his years as an RAF airman during the war and later amusing escapades in the UK and Egypt. *A very entertaining read.* **£9.95**

Beaufighters BOAC & Me • WW2 Beaufighter navigator **Sam Wright** served a full tour with 254 Sqn and was later seconded to BOAC on early postwar overseas routes. *'Captures the spirit of the mighty Beaufighter'* **£9.95**

Carried on the Wind • **Sean Feast** tells the fascinating story of Ted Manners, a 'special duties operator' with 101 Squadron, whose job was to 'spoof' enemy radar and intercept their surface-to-air radio messages in WW2. **£9.95**

Coastal Command Pilot • Former Hudson pilot **Ted Rayner**'s outstanding account of his unusual WW2 Coastal Command experiences, flying in the Arctic from bases in Iceland and Greenland. **£9.95**

Cyril Wild: The Tall Man Who Never Slept • **James Bradley**'s biography of a remarkable Japanese-speaking British Army officer who helped many POWs survive at Sonkurai Camp on the infamous Burma railway. **£9.95**

Desert War Diary • **John Walton's** diary and photos record the activities of the Hurricanes and personnel of 213 Squadron during WW2 in Cyprus and Egypt. *"Informative and entertaining."* **£9.95**

Espionage Behind the Wire • former POW **Howard Greville** tells the fascinating story of how he worked as a spy for British intelligence (MI6) from inside a German POW camp. **£9.95**

From Fiji to Balkan Skies • Spitfire/Mustang pilot **Dennis McCaig** recalls eventful WW2 operations over the Adriatic/Balkans with 249 Sqn in 43/44. *'A rip-roaring real-life adventure, splendidly written.'* **£9.95**

Get Some In! • The many wartime adventures of **Mervyn Base**, a WW2 RAF Bomb Disposal expert **£9.95**

Hunt Like a Tiger • **Tom Docherty** an illustrated history of 230 squadron – equipped during the war with Sunderland flying boats which were put to many uses in many theatres of war. A fascinating piece of RAF history. **£9.95**

Just a Survivor • Former Lancaster navigator **Phil Potts** tells his remarkable tale of survival against the odds in the air with 103 Sqn and later as a POW. *'An enlightening and well written account.'* **£9.95**

Memoirs of a 'Goldfish' • The eventful wartime memoirs of former 115 Sqn Wellington pilot **Jim Burtt-Smith**, now president of the Goldfish Club - exclusively for aviators who have force-landed into water. **£9.95**

Nobody Unprepared • The history of No 78 Sqn RAF is told in full for the first time by **Vernon Holland** in this absorbing account of the Whitley/Halifax squadron's World War 2 exploits. Full statistics and roll of honour. **£14.95**

No Brylcreem, No Medals • RAF MT driver **Jack Hambleton** 's splendid account of his wartime escapades in England, Shetlands & Middle East blends comic/tragic aspects of war in uniquely entertaining way. **£9.95**

Nobody's Hero • Former RAF Policeman **Bernard Hart-Hallam**'s extraordinary adventures with 2TAF Security Section on D-Day and beyond in France, Belgium & Germany. *"Unique and frequently surprising."* **£9.95**

Operation Pharos • **Ken Rosam** tells the story of the RAF's secret bomber base/staging post on the Cocos Keeling islands during WW2 and of many operations from there. *'A fascinating slice of RAF history.'* **£9.95**

Over Hell & High Water • WW2 navigator **Les Parsons** survived 31 ops on Lancasters with 622 Sqn, then went on to fly Liberators in Far East with 99 Sqn. *'An exceptional tale of 'double jeopardy'.* **£9.95**

Pacifist to Glider Pilot • The son of Plymouth Brethren parents, **Alec Waldron** renounced their pacifism and went on to pilot gliders with the Glider Pilot Regiment at both Sicily & Arnhem. *Excellent photos.* **£9.95**

Pathfinder Force Balkans • Pathfinder F/Engineer **Geoff Curtis** saw action over Germany & Italy before baling out over Hungary. He was a POW in Komarno, Stalags 17a & 17b. *'An amazing catalogue of adventures.'* **£9.95**

Per Ardua Pro Patria • Humour and tragedy are interwoven in these unassuming autobiographical observations of **Dennis Wiltshire**, a former Lancaster Flight Engineer who later worked for NASA. **£9.95**

Ploughs, Planes & Palliasses • Entertaining recollections of RAF pilot **Percy Carruthers**, who flew Baltimores in Egypt with 223 Squadron and was later a POW at Stalag Luft 1 & 6. **£9.95**

RAF/UXB The Story of RAF Bomb Disposal • Stories contributed by wartime RAF BD veterans that will surprise and educate the uninitiated. *"Amazing stories of very brave men."* **£9.95**

Railway to Runway • Wartime diary & letters of Halifax Observer **Leslie Harris** – killed in action with 76 Sqn in 1943 – poignantly capture the spirit of the wartime RAF in the words of a 20-year-old airman. **£9.95**

Seletar Crowning Glory • The history of the RAF base in Singapore from its earliest beginnings, through the golden era of the flying-boats, its capture in WW2 and on to its closure in the 1970s. **£15.00**

The RAF & Me • Former Stirling navigator **Gordon Frost** recalls ops with 570 Sqn from RAF Harwell, including 'Market-Garden' 'Varsity' and others. *'A salute to the mighty Stirling and its valiant crews.'* **£9.95**

Training for Triumph • **Tom Docherty**'s very thorough account of the amazing achievement of RAF Training Command, who trained over 90,000 aircrew during World War 2. *'An impressively detailed book.'* **£12.00**

To Strive and Not to Yield • An inspiring account of the involvement of No 626 Squadron RAF Bomber Command in the 'Battle of Berlin' (1943/44) and a salute to the men and women who served on the squadron. **£14.95**

Un Grand Bordel • Geoffrey French relates air-gunner **Norman Lee**'s amazing real-life adventures with the French Maquis (Secret Army) after being shot down over Europe. *"Frequently funny and highly eventful."* **£9.95**

UXB Vol 2 • More unusual and gripping tales of bomb disposal in WW2 and after. **£9.95**

Wot! No Engines? • Alan Cooper tells the story of military gliders in general and the RAF glider pilots who served on Operation Varsity in 1945 in particular. A very large and impressive book with many photos. **£18.00**

While Others Slept • Former Hampden navigator **Eric Woods** tells the story of Bomber Command's early years and how he completed a tour of duty with 144 Squadron. *'Full of valuable historical detail.'* **£9.95**

WOMEN & WORLD WAR TWO

A WAAF at War • Former MT driver **Diana Lindo**'s charming evocation of life in the WAAF will bring back happy memories to all those who also served in World War 2. *"Nostalgic and good-natured."* **£9.95**

Corduroy Days • Warm-hearted and amusing recollections of **Josephine Duggan-Rees**'s wartime years spent as a Land Girl on farms in the New Forest area. *"Funny, nostalgic and very well written."* **£9.95**

Ernie • **Celia Savage**'s quest to discover the truth about the death of her father, an RAF Halifax navigator with 149 Sqn, who died in WW2 when she was just 6 years old. *"A real-life detective story."* **£9.95**

In My Father's Footsteps • **Pat Bienkowski**'s moving account of her trip to Singapore & Thailand to visit the places where her father and uncle were both POW's during WW2. **£9.95**

Lambs in Blue • **Rebecca Barnett's** revealing account of the wartime lives and loves of a group of WAAFs posted to the tropical paradise of Ceylon. *"A highly congenial WW2 chronicle."* **£9.95**

Radar Days • Delightful evocation of life in the wartime WAAF by former Radar Operator **Gwen Arnold**, who served at Bawdsey Manor RDF Station, Suffolk. *"Amusing, charming and affectionate."* **£9.95**

Searching in the Dark • The amusing wartime diary of **Peggy Butler** a WAAF radar operator 1942-1946 – written when she was just 19 yrs old and serving at Bawdsey RDF station in Suffolk **£9.95**

Tales of a Bomber Command Waaf (and her horse) • very entertaining book composed mainly of wartime letters received and sent by **Sylvia Pickering**, who served as a Waaf at RAF Cottesmore and RAF Coningsby. **£9.95**

More Tales of a Bomber Command Waaf (and her horse) • The second part of **Sylvia Pickering**'s war was spent at RAF Coningsby and HQ 5 Group (Bomber Command) at Morton Hall. Many more entertaining reminiscences. **£9.95**

Why Did We Join? • In this entertaining book **Eileen Smith** recalls the camaraderie, excitement and heartbreak of working as a Waaf on an operational Bomber Command Station – RAF East Kirkby in Lincolnshire. **£9.95**

MEMOIRS & HISTORIES – NON-MILITARY

A Beat Around the Bush • **Alastair Tompkins** recounts a variety of his extraordinary experiences– many of them very amusing indeed – as a Bush Policeman in British Colonial Kenya, 1952-62. Very entertaining. **£9.95**

20th CenturyFarmers Boy • Sussex farmer **Nick Adames** looks back on a century of rural change and what it has meant to his own family and the county they have farmed in for 400 years. **£9.95**

Call an Ambulance! • former ambulance driver **Alan Crosskill** recalls a number of light-hearted episodes from his eventful career in the 1960s/70s. *'Very amusing and entertaining'.* **£9.95**

Harry – An Evacuee's Story • The misadventures of **Harry Collins** – a young lad evacuated from his home in Stockport UK to Manitoba, Canada in WW2. *'An educational description of the life of an evacuee'* **£9.95**

Just Visiting • Charming and funny book by former Health Visitor **Molly Corbally**, who brilliantly depicts colourful characters and entertaining incidents from her long career. **£9.95**

Occupation Nurse • **Peter & Mary Birchenall** pay tribute to the achievement of the group of untrained nurses who provided healthcare at Guernsey's only hospital during the German occupation of 1940-45. **£9.95**

The JFK Assassination: Dispelling the Myths • Prepare to revise everything you thought you knew about the most famous assassination of the 20th Century. British historian **Mel Ayton** examines the many 'myths' that have grown up in the 40 years since JFK was murdered and debunks them all. You may be surprised at his conclusions. **£9.95**

FICTION

A Trace of Calcium by **David Barnett** • A commuter comes to the aid of a young woman in trouble, becomes implicated in murder and must use all his resources to clear his name. (contains sex & violence) **£9.95**

Double Time by **David Barnett** • A light-hearted time-travel fantasy in which a bookmaker tries to use a time machine to make his fortune and improve his love-life with hilarious consequences. (contains sex & violence) **£9.95**

Dust & Fury by **David Barnett** • An epic family saga set in the Sultanate of Oman, featuring the lives and loves of an Omani family during the bitter war that led to the foundation of modern Oman. (contains sex & violence) **£15.00**

The Brats • this very entertaining novel by **Tony Paul** is based on the true story of his grandfather, who as a boy along with several friends, stowed away on a ship bound for Canada. The youngsters' brutal mistreatment at the hands of the Captain and Mate of the ship caused a scandal that made headlines in Victorian times. **£9.95**

The Cherkassy Incident by **Hunter Carlyle** Terrorists plot to steal nuclear missiles from a sunken Russian nuclear submarine; can an international team of security agents stop them? (contains sex & violence) **£9.95**

BOOKS FEATURING THE SOUTH COAST & THE SOUTH DOWNS REGION

A Portrait of Slindon • **Josephine Duggan Rees** has written a charming history of this attractive and well-preserved West Sussex village, from its earliest beginnings to the present day, taking in the exploits of its many notable residents over the years. Very informative and entertaining. Illustrated with many photos, some in colour. **£14.95**

Retribution • **Mike Jupp** has created an outrageous and very funny comedy/fantasy novel for adults and older children, featuring bizarre goings-on in a fictional quiet English seaside town that bears a striking resemblance to Mike's home town of Bognor Regis. Brilliantly illustrated. *One of the funniest books you will ever read.* **£9.95**

Unknown to History and Fame • **Brenda Dixon**'s charming portrait of Victorian life in the West Sussex village of Walberton via the writings of Charles Ayling, a resident of the village, whose reports on local events were a popular feature in *The West Sussex Gazette* over many years during the Victorian era. **£9.95**

A Little School on the Downs • **Mary Bowmaker** tells the amazing story of Harriet Finlay-Johnson, headmistress of a little village school in Sompting, West Sussex in the 1890s, whose ideas and classroom techniques began a revolution in education. She also scandalised society at the time by marrying a former pupil, 20 years her junior. **£9.95**

The South Coast Beat Scene of the 1960s The South Coast may not have been as famous as Liverpool in the swinging sixties but it was nevertheless a hotbed of musical activity. Broadcaster **Mike Read** traces the complete history of the musicians, the fans and the venues from Brighton to Bognor in this large and lavishly-illustrated book. **£24.95**

Boys & Other Animals • **Josephine Duggan Rees**'s warm-hearted and delightfully funny account of a mother's many trials and tribulations bringing up a boisterous all-male family on a farm in rural Sussex during the 1950s-70s. **£9.95**

Woodfield books are available direct from the publishers by mail order

Telephone your orders to (+44 if outside UK) **01243** 821234

Fax orders your to (+44 if outside UK) **01243** 821757

Write to: Book Orders, Woodfield Publishing, Bognor Regis, West Sussex PO21 5EL

All major credit cards accepted Please make cheques payable to 'Woodfield Publishing'.

Visit our website for up-to-date details of our latest titles and special offers. Secure online purchasing is also available

at: **www.woodfieldpublishing.com**